轮机员应对船东面试英语

主　编：吴雪花

副主编：陈　蓓　蒋更红

东南大学电子音像出版社

·南京·

内容提要

《轮机员应对船东面试英语》是适应 STCW2010 马尼拉修正案的船员英语交流的新要求及船员外派等形势应运而生的辅助教材。包括应对面试小贴士,常见问题及口述题,并提供参考答案,必要处配有注释,常用词汇,面试实例及录音。内容涉及个人信息,船员资历,船舶认识,基本安全,应急情况,法律法规,轮机业务知识,轮机员基本职责与机舱资源管理。适用对象为航海院校学生、社会船员、从事轮机英语教学的工作者。

轮机员应对船东面试英语

出版发行	东南大学电子音像出版社
出 版 人	江建中
责任编辑	史建农
社　　址	江苏省南京市玄武区四牌楼 2 号
邮　　编	210096

销售电话	(025)83792327/83794561/83794174/83794121/ 83795802/57711295(传真)
网　　址	http://www. seupress. com
经　　销	江苏省新华书店
印　　刷	南京玉河印刷厂
开　　本	850 mm×1168 mm　1/32
印　　张	4
字　　数	105 千字
书　　号	ISBN 978 - 7 - 900714 - 96 - 1
版　　次	2012 年 7 月第 1 版
印　　次	2012 年 7 月第 1 次印刷
定　　价	29.00 元(含附册)

(本社图书若有印装质量问题,请直接与营销部联系,电话:025 - 83791830)

前　言

　　《轮机员应对船东面试英语》是适应STCW2010马尼拉修正案的船员英语交流的新要求及船员外派等形势应运而生的辅助教材。一直以来,虽然中国船员业务能力强,苦干能服从命令,但由于英语交流能力落后等原因,外派率较低。为了改变这种状况,编者结合实际参与面试的培训经历,邀请企业中有丰富经验的船长和轮机长参与编写和审稿工作,使此书具有前瞻性、实用性、专业性强等特点。相信此书能帮助学员摆脱"哑巴英语",揭开船东面试的面纱,克服心理障碍,通过认真研读与操练,使自己的英语听说能力能上一个台阶,顺利应对船东英语面试。

　　本书的适用对象为航海院校轮机工程专业学生、社会船员、从事轮机英语教学的工作者。

　　此书包括了应对面试小贴士,常见问题及口述题,并提供参考答案,必要处配有注释,常用词汇,面试实例及录音。内容涉及个人信息,船员资历,船舶认识,基本安全,应急情况,法律法规,轮机业务知识,轮机员基本职责与机舱资源管理。本书的宗旨是为学院和企业培养英语能力强的外派船员,为促进船员劳务市场的发展做点力所能及的事。

　　参与本书编写的老师来自江苏海事职业技术学院、青岛远洋船员职业学院和浙江交通职业技术学院。赵丹老师参与了第一章、第五章部分内容的编写工作。刘婷婷老师参与了第三章、第五章部分内容的编写工作。吴雪花老师参与了第四章、第六章的编写并承担全书的策划工作。蒋更红老师参与了面试实例的编写工作。陈蓓、王春和林红老师参与了录音工作。本书由实践和面试经验丰富的王红兵轮机长及南京远腾船务有限公司周卓平船长参与了审稿工作。

　　书中难免会存在疏漏的地方,惠请国内外同行、专家和广大读者提出宝贵修改意见。

　　如有疑问,可咨询主编吴雪花老师。

　　信箱:wuxuehua2001@sina.com

2012年6月

目 录

Chapter 5 Professional Knowledge about Marine Engineering

Chapter 6 Crew's Duties and Knowledge about Engine Room Resources Management

Chapter 1　Personal Information and Experiences

第 1 章　个人信息与船员资历

Tips

　　见到船东时应向船东打招呼、礼貌(Polite)、简洁(Concise)、热情(Enthusiastic)。面试前留给船东的第一印象往往是刚刚与船东见面时留下的。经验告诉我们,很多船员尽管英文不错,可是往往不知道如何和船东恰当地打招呼,从而影响了自己的面试成绩。其实,最常见的打招呼办法就很有效。进考官面试房间后,切勿长时间东张西望,而要在外派公司的引导人员的示意下,坐到指定的座位上。然后,通常是由外派公司的人员互相介绍你和面试你的船东。在介绍完后,你要向考官主动打一下招呼,说一声"你好!"或"How do you do?"及"I am John, very glad to meet you here"。这里要提醒的是,你落座后,一定要看看对面坐着几位考官。在打招呼时,要和每个人打招呼,包括身体主动前倾,和每个人握握手,或有礼貌地和每个人点点头。千万不能忘了其中的一个或几个。在打完招呼后,要回到指定的座位,端庄坐下。坐下后,通常船东考官会首先向你提出问题,要你回答。

　　若对方没有立即向你提问题,你可以自己首先打破僵局,最好的方法是主动介绍一下自己,如果外派公司已经把你介绍给考官了,你在自我介绍时要介绍那些别人介绍你时没有向考官提供的信息,比如你的职位、你的姓名、你来自中国的哪个省份或城市等等,但自我介绍时,要言简意赅,切忌长篇大论。

　　主动热情地和考官交流会使自己易于被考官接受和喜欢。一般认为,热情是做好一项工作的非常重要的前提条件之一。但是,热情要有度,开放自己的精神空间也要有度。面试的背景要求考官和考生之间要有一定的距离。如果考生和考官过于亲密,容易让人产生动机不纯或交际态度不稳重的看法。想与考官"见面熟"的急于求成的做法是不妥当的。既要主动接近,又要保持一定的距离,这就是"热情"的全面含义。

　　常用的寒暄语有:

　　Nice to meet you! /It's very nice to meet you! /Glad to meet you! /Pleased to meet you! /A pleasure to meet you!

　　对于以前见过的老朋友,可以说:

　　How are you? /How is going?

1.1　个人信息 Personal Information

　　船员的个人信息包括:家庭信息、教育背景、持有的证书、对工作的期望值和对未来的计划等方面。一个准备充分的船员,会在面试之前对自己的个人信息进行整理,并找出在这信息中的闪光点,在面试之前组织好语言,面试的时候,就能做到从容不迫,有条不紊。下面就列举可能会出现的一些问题:

Part I　Questions

1. What is your name?

Could you tell me your name?

Could you tell me what is your name?

Your name?

I am Wang Ming/My name is Wang Ming

2. What Certificate of Competency do you hold?

I hold the Chief Engineer's Certificate. /I hold the Second Engineer's Certificate. /I hold the Third Engineer's Certificate. /I hold the Fourth Engineer's Certificate.

3. Do you have a Duty Watch Certificate issued by MSA?

   Yes, I have./No, I haven't.

4. How long have you served COSCO?

   I have served COSCO for 10 years.

5. How many harbors have you ever been to?

   I have been to many harbors, such as Shanghai, London, Yokohama, Hamburg, New York and so on.

6. What port did you often call at?

   I often called at Shanghai, Singapore.

7. What port do you prefer? What port do you dislike?

   I like Singapore very much. It is very clean and beautiful.

8. How many countries have you ever been to? Which country do you like best?

   I have been to England, Japan, Singapore and so on. I like Singapore more.

9. How long have you worked on board?

   One year/two years.

10. Please briefly introduce yourself(as a deck/engine cadet) to us. Or tell us something about yourself.

   I am an engineer cadet, and I graduated from Shanghai Maritime University.

11. Please tell me what major you had in the marine university/college/school?

   Marine engineering.

12. What courses(subjects) have you learned during your studies there? Which courses do you like most? Why?

   Marine Engineering English, Marine Propulsion Diesel Engine, Auxiliary Machinery, Automation, Ship Management, Electrical Equipment and so on. I like English very much, because it is

very important for my future work and our English teacher is very
kind to us.

13. Why do you want to be a sailor? Are you willing to work hard?
How long do you want to be a sailor? Do you have any friend as a
seaman? What do you know about seaman's life?
I like sea very much. I can go to many countries free of charge.
And I can earn a lot of money. I am willing to work hard because
I come from the countryside and my family is poor. I want to
work on board for more than 15 years if everything goes well. I
learn about sea life from my neighbor, he is a sailor.

14. What other plans do you have for the coming 5 or 6 years?
I want to be the second engineer in 5 or 6 years.

15. Do you think that sailing is a very ideal job for you? Could your
brother follow your step?
Yes, sailing is an ideal job for me. I can enjoy the sunset and
sunrise everyday, and I can go to many countries free of charge.
I think I will do my work well under the second engineer's and
chief engineer's instructions.

16. If Capt(C/E) scold you, will you fight back? Why?
No. We will communicate with each other and talk about some
disputes.

17. Have you got a girlfriend? If you have, will you miss your
girlfriend?
Yes, I have a girlfriend. I will miss her. But she supports my
job.

18. When do you want to get married?
I think I will not marry soon, since my family think I should
spend more time on work these years.

19. Do you have hobbies? What hobbies do you like best, why?
I like playing basketball./I like ping pong best.

20. Which country do you like best?

I like our country best! You know, as China made great progresses these years, Our Chinese can be very proud of her!

21. Do you smoke or drink?

Yes, I can drink a little. But I seldom drink when I am on board. But I don't smoke.

(According to the ISM, the BAC shall not be more than 0.04% by weight any time when being tested. But watch keepers are not allowed to drink any alcoholic beverage 4 hours before their watch.)

22. What is your favorite sport?

I like basketball most.

23. Do you have the watch-keeping license? 你有没有值班证书?

Yes, I do.

注:通常来说,船上的 BOSUN,AB 等职位要操舵值班,具备 STCW1978/2010 公约下的值班证书很重要。

24. How many years have you worked as No. 1 oiler? When did you start work as a seaman? How many ships have you worked as No. 1 oiler? 干几年机工长了? 什么时候开始干船员的? 做过几条船的机工长?

For five years. I started to work as a seaman ten years ago. I have worked as a No. 1 oiler(chief motorman) for four ships.

25. What's your English proficiency?

I have passed CET-Band 6(or 4). I like English very much and I can communicate with foreigners well.

26. If you are asked to do a lot of work on ship, will you have some complaint?

I think I won't. It depends on the job assignment. If it is the job under my responsibility and I can manage it, I will have no complaint. But if the work is too hard and too much for me, I think I will discuss with my superiors and find a good method to settle it. Anyway, I will not quarrel with my superiors, instead I will try my best to communicate with him and find methods to solve any problems.

27. What position do you apply for?

I am applying for the 4/E position in your company.

28. What education degree do you have?

I have a bachelor's degree/associate degree.

29. Which classification society is your ship registered with?

Our ship is registered with China Classification Society.

30. Can you introduce your hometown?

Yes. I was born in a small town in Yangzhou. It is very beautiful. It is famous for ducks and lakes.

31. Would you like to work with seamen from different countries?

Yes, I love to. My English is good and I have learned a lot about different cultures. I think I can get along well with foreigners. And the most important, we can learn from each other.

32. Can you introduce your school?

Yes, Sir. Our Institute is a specialized maritime vocational institute. It is very big and beautiful.

33. Do you have any idea about our company/Why do you choose our company?

I learned about your company from our schoolmate and I searched it from the internet. Your company is very famous and I can have a lot of chances of learning and promotion.

Part II Topics

1. Self-introduction(for reference)

My name is Wang Xin. I am 20 years old. Now I am studying in Jiangsu Maritime Institute. My major is marine engineering and I will become an engineer after graduation. I have ever worked on the training ship of our college and learned a lot from the working experience. There are three members in my family, my father, mother and I. My parents love me very much and they hope that I will become a skillful engineer in the future.

2. Say something about your work experience.

I have worked on a bulk carrier named MV "Star", 80,000 gross tonnage with 5 holds. The ports we often called are in European. I worked on this ship as a 4/E for about 10 months. I worked as a 3/E on a tanker ship. I enjoy my work and like to stay with my colleagues.

Commonly used phrases

MSA(Maritime Safety Administration) 海事安全管理局

Important canals all over the world: the Grand Canal in China, the Suez Canal, the Panama Canal and the Kiel Canal.

Important harbors: Amsterdam 阿姆斯特丹,荷兰

Rotterdam 鹿特丹,荷兰

Manila 马尼拉,菲律宾

Osaka 大阪,日本

Sydney 悉尼,澳大利亚

1.2 船员资历 Experiences of the seafarers

Tips

船东对船员的资历特别感兴趣,他想了解你服务过的船舶类型、主机和副机类型,你在船上遇到的故障及排除方法等。所以船员在面试前可搜索一下以前服务过的船舶情况、个人经历等,以便积极应对船东提出的有关资历方面的问题。

Part Ⅰ Questions

1. How long have you worked on board?

I have worked on board for 10 years.

2. What ports do you often call?

We often call at Japanese harbors, such as Tokyo, Yokohama.

3. What certificate do you have?

I have the C/E's Certificate.

4. Have you served as chief engineer \ second engineer \ third engineer \ fourth engineer \ No. 1 oiler \ motorman \ pumpman \ wiper \ storeman?

Yes, I have served as second engineer for several years/for a short time.

No, I am sorry, I hold a C/E's certificate, but I have never worked as a chief engineer.

5. What kind of ship have you worked on?

I have worked on many kinds of ships, such as bulk carriers, passenger ship, tanker, and so on.

船舶的种类有：dry cargo ship(干货船)，liquid cargo ship(液体货船)，passenger ship(客轮)and fishing ship(渔船)，etc.

6. Can you tell me something about your last ship?

It was a bulk carrier, named Dong Fang and 10 years old. It usually sails at the south-east Asia.

7. Do you have a Seaman's Book?

Yes, I have.

8. Do you have a passport?

Yes, I have.

9. Do you have worked on any foreign ships and worked with any foreign seafarers?

Yes, I have worked on a Singapore ship with some seafarers from European countries.

10. Do you have any experience on UMS?

I have worked on UMS, and the main engine can be controlled

from the bridge. It is equipped with modern machines.

11. What was your trade area for your last ship?

My last ship was an ocean-going vessel, and we often visited North America, European ports, and so on.

12. Is there any difficulty for you to work on a multinational crew ship?

No, I don't think so. I am good at English and have learned different cultures.

13. Could you tell me some types of main engine you have worked on?

I have worked on board with main engine of Sulzer, MAN-B&W, and UEC etc.

14. What kind of auxiliary engine have you served?

I have served auxiliary engine Yanmar, Daihatsu.

15. Have you ever met any emergency conditions on board ship?

No, I haven't./Yes, I have met a very rough sea when our ship was travelling in the Pacific Ocean. The No. 1 cylinder of the main engine stopped working suddenly when I kept on watch. I informed the bridge immediately and sounded the alarm. Then we took some emergency actions according to the emergency plan, and the main engine restored to normal working condition.

Part II Topics

1. Do you have any plans for your seafarer life?

Right now, I say, I will serve the job permanently. I want to be a Chief Engineer in my working life. So I think I will work hard in the future, if I have the chance to get this job.

2. Your daily work on board

(1) Your position on board.

(2) Your duties on board.

(3) Your experiences.

I'm a fourth engineer. I usually work in the engine room. Every day, I am on duty from 8 to 12 both in the morning and in the evening. During my watch, I do cleaning, maintenance and repair work. It's my duty to keep every machine in the engine room in good order. I have worked on many kinds of bulk carriers.

3. Have you met the main engine breakdown cases? Describe briefly you experienced.

One night when I was on duty in the engine room, I found that the main engine running with one cylinder not working. I reported it to the chief engineer and bridge immediately.

First, we prevented the diesel engine from being overloaded. In order to achieve that, we reduced its revolution. Secondly, regulated the main engine revolution to avoid turbocharger continuous surging. Thirdly, we took some measures to avoid engine vibration. In order to sail safely we were more careful to check the main engine, finally we found out the engine trouble, the puncture valve of the fuel pump was stuck on the open position, we solved the trouble, main engine restored to normal working condition.

4. Have you ever worked on multinational crew ship? Is there any difficulty?

Yes! I have met some difficulties when I first worked with the foreign crews especially when they are from different countries. You know, the main reason is just because of the language. But now, I have no difficulties in language any more, since my English is very good now, and I have learned different cultures and I can get on well with all my colleagues.

Commonly used phrases

    bosun 水手长

    carpenter 木匠

    quarter master 舵工

    AB：able bodied 一水

    OS：ordinary seaman 二水

    No. 1 oiler 机工长

    motorman 机工

Chapter 2　Knowledge about Basic Safety, Emergency Conditions and Familiarization with Ships

第2章　基本安全、应急情况知识和熟悉船舶

2.1　基本安全 Basic safety

Tips

　　船员在从事海上工作之前,就已经进行了相关的行业培训,消防、救生、工作安全等基本安全培训。研究表明,目前海上事故95%是人为因素导致的,遵守基本安全管理操作,是船员乃至船舶公司在运营过程中不可或缺的部分。本节就面试过程中,船上的指挥操作、人身、作业等方面的问题进行介绍。

Part Ⅰ　Questions

1. Who is responsible for the safety of the whole ship?
   The captain is responsible for the safety of the whole ship.
2. How often do you have a safety meeting on board?
   Once a month.
3. How often do you carry out a fire fighting drill? Who controls on the spot?

Once a month. In the engine department, the chief engineer will control on the spot.

Fire fighting drill

Life saving drill

Abandon ship drill

Emergency fire pump

4. How often do you have a boat drill or fire drill?

Once a month.

5. How often should the emergency fire pump be started?

Once a week.

6. How to test the emergency fire pump?

Usually the emergency pump is driven by an electrical motor or a diesel engine. If the pump is driven by diesel engine, before starting, you should check the engine also. Usually the emergency fire pump is a centrifugal pump, before starting, the pump inlet valves should be opened, and then you can start the pump, and open the discharge valve when the discharge pressure has been built up, normally more than $5kgs/cm^2$. We should start it once a week and keep it running for at least 3 minutes.

7. What basic safety training shall all crewmembers receive?
Basic First Aid, Personal Survival, Basic Fire Fighting, Personal Safety/Social Responsibilities.

8. When shall an abandon ship drill be carried out for a passenger ship?
Usually within 24 hours after ship's sailing.

9. Who is responsible for operating lifeboat engine?
The fourth engineer.

10. What should be done before carbon dioxide is released to the engine room?
Before carbon dioxide is released, the alarm should be given and all the crew in the engine room must leave right away and close all the doors and windows, stop the generators, start the emergency generator, release steam pressure in the auxiliary boiler, shut all quick closing valves for oil tanks, stop all ventilations, etc..

11. How do you put it out when you come across the fire caused by electrical equipment?
Switch off the power source at first and then put it out with a carbon dioxide extinguisher.

12. When the fire alarm is sounded continuously, what should the engine room personnel do?
Evacuate from the engine room and gather to their own positions according to the muster list.

13. Where can you see the muster list on your ship?
We can see the muster list on the bridge, in the engine control

room, on the avenue wall, on the meeting room wall and some other important places.

14. What can you see on the muster list?

Various alarm signals, the muster station, emergency duties and so on.

15. What should pay attention to when you enter the enclosed space?

I should pay attention to the density of air in this enclosed space, and if there is explosive air in this space.

16. Who is in charge of emergency generator?

The second engineer.

17. What is your emergency position on the Muster List when abandon ship? （注意：不同状况下职责是不同的，有消防、弃船、救人等）

Basically, I am supposed to control and operate the lifeboat engine.

18. How do you put it out when you come across the fire caused by oil?

I should use a foam extinguisher to put out the oil fire.

19. How do you treat the injured person who is not breathing?

I should let him lie on a hard surface and give him first aid treatment, such as artificial respiration or mouth-to-mouth measure.

20. How do you deal with the chemicals in the E/R?

We always stow the chemicals in the well-ventilated spaces and post the notice & MSDS nearby.

21. What measures do you usually take to keep the E/R clean?

We do cleaning work in the engine room every watch. All the leaks should be detected and rectified in time.

22. Tell me something about Fire Fighting Equipment you know.

Fixed installations include fire pumps, fire hydrant, emergency fire pump, fixed CO_2 release system, and international shore connections. Portable(moveable) fire extinguishers: foam extinguisher, CO_2 extinguisher, dry powder extinguisher.

23. What are the three factors for combustion?

Oxygen, heat and combustibles(air, heat and fuel).

24. What classifications can fire be divided into and their correspondent extinguishing medium?

Class A: solid materials	A < < < water
Class B: liquids	A&B < < < Foam
Class C: gas and electricity	B&C < < < CO_2
Class D: combustible metals	D < < < dry chemical

25. What fire fighting apparatus have you got on board?

Water spray system, fireman's outfit, fire-proof doors, fire damper, fire pump, all kinds of extinguishers, fire hose, hydrant, axes and so on.

26. How many basic ways of fire fighting do you know?

They are isolating mode, smothering mode, cooling mode and chemical inhibiting mode.

27. For what kind of fire is the foam extinguisher the most effective?

It is most effective to put out oil fire.

28. How do you put out an electrical equipment fire?

To cut off the electricity supply first, then put out the fire with dry powder or CO_2 extinguisher.

29. Why can't we put out electrical equipment fire with foam extinguisher?

Because foam conducts electricity. It will cause short circuit and make someone get electric shock/shot.

30. What are the life-saving appliances?

They are lifeboat, rescue boat, life raft, life buoy, immersion suit and life jacket.

31. What does the emergency equipment include?

It includes the emergency fire pump, emergency generator, switchboard and batteries, emergency air compressor and emergency steering gear. It may also include some quick-closing gears of skylight and ventilator.

32. What does the personal protective equipment refer to?

It refers to safety helmet, safety overall, eye and ear protection, gloves, safety belt and safety working shoes(boots) etc.

33. What measures should be taken when welding is being done in the welding room?

Get some fire-fighting equipment and welding protection apparatus ready and keep the room constant ventilating. Assign someone to keep watch.

34. What does SARE stand for?

It stands for search and rescue equipment.

35. Do you wear your gloves where you are working?

Yes, besides, I should always wear ear protectors, helmet, working uniform, and safety boots while I am watching in the engine room.

36. Before entering an enclosed space such as ballast tank, what action will you take?

Prepare tools. Check all items in the checklist, such as test of content of oxygen, test of radiation, test of explosion point, exploded-proof lamp, good ventilation before entering, communication means available between operators inside and watchman outside, and so on. Operators should wear protective clothing, breathing apparatus, helmet, working boots, and outfit such as lifeline, establishing a mark plate "Dangerous Operation in Progress" and so on.

37. Can you say the colors of the permanent signs on your ship?

There are four colors for these signs: red, yellow, blue and green.

38. What will be paid attention to when bunkering fuel oil?

Firstly, we must pay much attention not to spill oil; secondly, the quantity of the oil must correspond to the contract; thirdly the quality must comply with the required one; fourthly, we must take samples during bunkering.

39. How can you keep the seafarers energy?

They should have a good rest after their work and the rest time in a day should not be less than 10 hours a day and 70 hours a week.

40. How will you ensure the seafarers are not fatigued?

We make them have a good rest. At the same time, we provide good food nutrition, good sleeping and make them in good mood.

41. How do you deal with chemicals on board?

We should deal with chemicals according to MSDS (Material Safety Data Sheet).

42. Where should the additional lifejackets put?

In the workplace, like bridge, bosun store, Engine Control Room.

43. What does "Permit-to-Work mean?"

It is a checklist to develop a safe system for the job by reducing the hazard to a safe acceptable level. For example, if you want to work at height, or before welding and entering enclosed space, you should get "Permit-to-Work".

44. How do you understand "enclosed space"?

Enclosed space refers to oil storage tank, ballast tank, and space without ventilation.

45. You see someone doing welding work in E/R or on bridge, what should you do?

I should remind him to remove combustible materials, ensure good ventilation.

46. What is the reason for carrying out "Fire Safety Rounds?"

We should make rounds in the engine room to detect fire sources, check the electrical equipment to avoid fire accident.

47. How often will you test general emergency fire pump? （是通用消防泵,不是应急消防泵）

Once a week.

48. How often will you test general emergency alarm?

Once a week.

49. How often will you test the lifeboat engine?

Once a week.

50. You see someone working at height. What will you do?

I will remind him to wear safety belt and wear hardhat. Also I should wear safety helmet.

51. What is "EEBD"?

Emergency Escape Breathing Device（紧急逃生呼吸装置）

EEBD   Life boat

52. What precautions do you take when machinery is opened up for maintenance?

We should cut off electricity, post warning notice and safety line.

53. How many kinds of fire detectors are there?

Three: flame, smoke, and heat.

54. What personal safety equipment should be available at battery room, paint room, chemical storage space, lathe machine, and fixed grinder?

Battery room—gloves, glasses, waist cloth(围裙)

Paint room—gloves, glasses, explosion-proof torch light(防爆灯)

Chemical storage space—gloves, glasses, waist cloth

Lathe machine—goggles(护目镜)

Fixed grinder—goggles

Goggles   **Explosion-proof torch light**

55. You see oil/grease stains on deck/in the engine room, what will you do?

Remove it with sawdust or oil absorbent. Otherwise someone may slip, or it may cause fire.

Part II   Topics

1. Talk about the Muster List.

A Muster List should include the following points:

(1) Details of emergency alarm signal;

(2) How ship-abandon order will be given;

(3) The boat to which each person belongs and duties to be performed in an abandon ship situation;

（4）The specific group to which a person belongs and general duties during various emergencies;

（5）Any additional or specific duties;

（6）Specific assembly point of each group.

The Muster Lists must be ready before a ship sails. We had the following Muster Lists on board the last vessel: general emergency, fire fighting, fire in the engine, emergency steering, abandon-ship, man overboard and oil prevention station.

2. Describe briefly one of the cases that you experienced or heard about evacuating from the engine room.

One afternoon a collision occurred, the situation was serious. A lot of sea water flooded the engine room and it was out of control soon. Then we heard the "abandon ship order". We had to evacuate from the engine room. We took the following actions: start the emergency generator, stop boilers, release their pressure and seal them off, shut off the valves of fuel oil or lubricating oil tanks, secure all the ventilators and watertight doors. Finally we evacuated from the engine room with the engine room logbook. The escape routes must be free from obstruction and kept bright.

Commonly used phrases

foam extinguisher 泡沫灭火器

dry powder extinguisher 干粉灭火器

fatigue 疲劳

nutrition 营养

mood 情绪

muster list 应急部署表

2.2　应急情况 Emergency conditions

Tips

应急情况在船上随时发生，船员应根据公司的安全管理体系，做好应急情况的应对训练和快速反应，如定期进行消防、救生、急救、放艇、弃船演习，以减少人员和财产的损失。船东面试比较关注这方面的问题。

Part I　Questions

1. Do you have any emergency methods for your ship in emergency condition? And who is responsible for it?

Yes, we have emergency plan on our ship. The C/E is responsible for the engine department.

2. What is alarm signal for a man falling overboard?

The signal is three long blasts on the ship's whistle and general alarm system.

3. What is the alarm signal for oil spill?

One short and two long and then one short sound alarm. This signal will be continued for about a minute.

4. How to treat flooding?

Sound alarm. Count all crew on board. Close all water tight doors and openings. Check damage and compare with vessel's stability. Use pumps or other means to eliminate or stop flooding. Transmit MAYDAY or PANPAN signal to ships in the vicinity. Check emergency power, main engine operation, and steering gear operation. Immediately decide to abandon or control the vessel. If abandon the ship, use abandoning ship procedure. Immediately report it to ship owner.

5. If a person overboard, what action should be taken?

Shout out man overboard for a crew first sighted. Continue to gaze the person in the water and throw a lifebuoy as clearly as possible to the person in the water. Report it to the bridge immediately. Sound the Oscar signal and hoist flag signal "O". Commence a Wiliamson turn(威廉姆森掉头,即朝人落水处打满舵,当转弯 60 度时回舵). Persons should use binoculars(双筒望远镜) if necessary. Inform the engine room to standby engine. Check the vessel's position. Standby rescue boat if necessary. If it occurs at night, searchlight should be used. If the person in the water is still unable to be found out, call for ships nearby for coordinated(合作的) search and rescue. If he is still missing, report to ship owner immediately.

6. In the event of collision, what should you do?

   If I'm on duty I should keep calm and operate the steering gear and main engine under the instructions of the bridge, then make preparations to pump out water.

7. What is the general emergency alarm signal?

   The signal is composed of seven short blasts followed by one long blast on the ship's whistle and general alarm system.

8. In the event of blackout, what should you do at first as a duty engineer?

   I should inform the chief engineer at once and then start the spare generator group.

9. In which cases the engineer should call the deck department?

   When there is anything that will affect the safety of the ship.

10. How do you evacuate from the engine room upon abandon ship order?

    We should first stop all the running equipment and close all the watertight doors and windows. Then start the emergency generator if possible(Usually the emergency generator will start automatically once the main switchboard loses power). At last, put on the life jacket and leave the E/R with the engine logbook.

11. How will you avoid an electric shock?

A severe electric shock may cause death, so it is very important to avoid electric shock. Before operating, we shall make sure that the power supply is switched off. Wear insulating gloves when working. Avoid touching capacitors or other components. Put on insulating shoes prior to working. If a long wire is used for feeding electricity, insulation of the sheath (护套、鞘) is required.

12. What are the causes of scavenge fires?

The scavenge fires may be caused by the wear of mechanical components, faulty fuel injection, inefficient exhaust system, incorrect cylinder lubricating oil leaks into scavenge space, insufficient drainage of scavenge drains, piston rings broken.

13. What can be done to prevent scavenge fires?

We should prevent the build-up of oil and sludge in the scavenge space, ensure the internal surface of the space kept reasonably clean, carry out routine piston ring inspections, ensure scavenge air temperature not above 55℃, ensure drains blown and clear and check fuel injection timing of each cylinder periodically.

14. What action will you take when scavenging fire occurs?

At first we should slow down the main engine and call the C/E and bridge. If the fire is not serious, we should do nothing but wait fire goes out itself. If the fire is very big, the main engine should be stopped, then the fire can be put out by the extinguisher which is equipped with the engine, normally we use the steam system on the engine side.

When the fire is put out, the problem has been solved; we can restore the engine running gradually. One thing you should pay more attention, the cylinder lube oil should be increased properly for the unit which gets the scavenging fire during the engine restoring period.

Part Ⅱ　Topics

1. Actions to be taken in the event of sudden stoppage of the main engine.

In the event of sudden stoppage of the main engine, we should report it to the chief engineer and the bridge immediately. Enter the engine room, try to find the cause.

If the oil pipe is broken and a great deal of oil is spilled out, we should replace the pipe and clean the spilt oil. Finally record it in the engine room log book.

2. Actions to be taken when scavenge fire occurs.

Once a fire is detected in the scavenge box, the engine should be slowed down, fuel shut off from the affected cylinder and cylinder lubrication increased to minimize the risk of seizure. All the scavenge drains should be closed. A small fire will be quickly burnt out, but where the fire persists, the engine must be stopped. A fire extinguishing agent should then be injected through the fitting provided in the scavenge box. Be sure that the box can't be opened.

3. Actions to be taken when a crankcase explosion occurs.

When crankcase explosion happens, first, we should slow the speed and ask the bridge for permission to stop. Secondly, we should leave the engine room unmanned with doors shut to avoid fresh air and prepare fire-fighting equipment. We shall also wait 20 minutes before entering the engine room for opening the crankcase door. After that, we should try to find out the source of the overheating. Finally after the repair work is completed, carry out crankcase inspections as usual. Don't forget to record in the engine logbook.

4. Actions to be taken when a fire occurs in the engine room.

When a fire occurs in the engine room, we should sound a fire alarm at first and report to the C/E. Then try to put out the fire with those portable extinguishers near the place where fire happened. If the fire burns heavily, we need to have that hatch sealed and release carbon dioxide. Before doing that, we should turn on the carbon dioxide alarm to ask all the engine department members to leave and then stop all engines in the engine room, shut all the doors, windows, skylights and ventilating pipes. At last release the carbon dioxide.

5. Actions to be taken in the event of collision.

When collision happens, the alarm signal should be sent out immediately and the chief engineer should come down to the engine room for the general command. Then the main engine should be operated correctly according to the bridge instructions. At last, the sounding of the oil and water tanks in the engine room should be taken and checked for leakage.

6. Actions taken in the event of blackout

When blackout occurs, we should start the emergency generator and supply power to lighting, navigational lights, steering gear and other equipment. We also should be careful, avoiding falling down from height or bumping against something. After the lighting system is on, we should try to find out the trouble.

注：也可这样回答 First, we should inform the bridge and start up the stand-by generator automatically to supply power. Secondly, we must take care not to fall from a height or bump against objects because the visibility decreases. Thirdly, we should try to find the cause for blackout. When the main switchboard resumes electric power, we should ensure that all necessary auxiliary machinery is restored in operation. Finally once normal operation is verified, inform the bridge and record in the engine logbook.

Commonly used phrases

　　alarm signal 警报

　　scavenge fire 扫气箱着火

　　electric shock 电击

　　collision 碰撞

　　emergency procedure 应急程序

　　search and rescue 搜救

2.3　熟悉船舶 Familiarization with ships

Tips

　　对于刚刚参加工作的船员来说，首先要对机舱有基本的了解。下面是面试时关于机舱的问题：

Part I　Questions

1. How many departments are there on board? What are they?

There are three departments on board. They are the Deck Department, the Engine Department and the Service(Catering) Department.

2. Please name the classes of the main engine.

Two-stroke main engine and four-stroke main engine.

3. A marine diesel engine consists of two parts. What are they?

Moving parts and fixed parts.

4. Please name three of the moving parts of a marine diesel engine.

Piston, connecting rod and crosshead.

5. What are the two types of cooling system in the engine room?

Fresh water cooling system and sea water cooling system.

6. The fuel oil system of a main engine can be divided into two sub-systems. What are they?

Fuel supply system and fuel injection system.

7. Lubricating oil is sometimes used for piston cooling. What's the advantage of this type of piston cooling?

The advantage is that any leakage of lube oil into the crankcase will not cause contamination.

8. The starting air pressure is too low. What should you do?

We should start the air compressor and pump up the air receiver.

9. Do you know who are in operational level?

Yes, of course. According to the STCW95, they include the second officer, the third engineer, the third officer and the fourth engineer.

10. Do you know who the ratings are?

Yes, of course. According to the STCW95, they are called support level seafarers. They include the bosun, carpenter, A. B. and O. S in the deck department and the No. 1 oiler, store man, oilers, motorman, pump man and wipers in the engine department. In the catering department, they are chief steward, chief cook, second cook, steward, boy, etc.

11. Who is responsible for the vessel?

The master/captain. He is responsible for the seaworthiness, efficient and economical operation of the vessel and management of the crew, cargo and ship borne equipment.

12. Do you know the ETA and ETD?

ETA refers to the estimated time of arrival; ETD is the estimated time of departure.

13. What does the full speed mean?

The full speed is the speed when the "ring off" engine is set. In general, it runs at economical speed.

14. What is the maneuvering speed?

The maneuvering speed is the speed which is less than the full speed. In general it is about 1/3 or 2/3 of the full speed. It's normally used for ship in/out harbors or sailing in narrow water course.

15. What is the canal speed?

The canal speed is the speed at which the vessel sails in the canal or in the narrow waters.

16. How do you maintain Emergency Battery?

I should fill in distilled water, or electrolyzed solution(电解液) if necessary and test the specific gravity periodically.

17. How do you heat the main engine?

I usually bring into operation of the heating system of the cooling water until the temperature of the cooling water returning from the jackets, liners and pistons is raised gradually to 60 ℃. The warming through period should extend over a period of about four hours.(或者可以这样说:I usually use the steam or generator engine cooling water to heat the main engine).

18. How do you operate the main engine in cold weather?

First we should warm up the engine before starting it. After starting it, we should keep it running at a low speed, and then increase the engine speed gradually to avoid combustion parts crack happening.

19. How do you change fuel oil into diesel oil?

Firstly, I lower the fuel oil temperature to a reasonable value. Open the diesel oil valve first, and then close the fuel oil valve. During the oil changing operation, I should pay more attention to the fuel oil system pressure to avoid engine trip due to fuel oil low pressure.

20. Why does the refrigerating compressor stops and starts frequently?

Low pressure controller differential set too close, leaky liquid line solenoid valve, lack of refrigerant, leakage between high and low chamber or dirty or iced evaporator.

21. What items of the main engine should you check before starting?

I should check that the fuel oil, lubricating oil and cooling water are at working level, check that all valves in the various systems are operational.

22. How does the duty engineer correct the clock in engine room?

The duty engineer should check the clock with the duty officer to ensure that the clock in the engine room is the same as the clock on the bridge.

23. Which machineries and control of spare parts should be in the charge of 2nd Engineer? (Which machineries and their spare parts should be charged by 2nd Engineer?)

Generator engine, fuel oil purifier, emergency generator, lifeboat engine, emergency fire pump, fuel oil control, deck machinery and others assigned by the chief engineer.

注:各公司对轮机员分管设备的规定有所不同。

24. What's a common trouble with a fuel pump plunger?

A common trouble with a fuel pump plunger is oil leakage.

25. What is the commonly used generator? (What kind of generator is commonly used?)

The AC generator is the commonly used one.

26. What machine can be used to generate power?

The four-stroke diesel engine.

27. Could you list different kinds of ship's survey?

The ship's survey may be Statutory Survey, Class Survey, annual survey, docking survey, intermediate survey, additional survey and so on.

28. What is the purpose of the Classification Society? Could you list some?

The Classification Society is to evaluate the condition of the ship, manage the shipping companies and the ships. It is nongovernment organization. The famous classification societies are: CCS(China), ABS(America), NK(Japan), DNV(Norwegian), BV(France) and the most famous one—LR(Lloyd's Register of Shipping).

29. What does CCR(ECR) refer to?

It refers to centralized control room (集控室)(Engine control room 机房控制室).

30. How many types of oils do you know?

Usually there are fuel, diesel and lube oil. Diesel oil is used for starting the main engine and maneuvering. Fuel oil is used when the ship sails at normal speed. Lube oil is used to reduce friction between moving parts, take away heat and wash away wear detritus.

31. What is critical speed?

The critical speed is the theoretical angular velocity(速度) which excites the natural frequency of a rotating object, such as a shaft, propeller, leadscrew, or gear. As the speed of rotation approaches the object's natural frequency, the object begins to resonate(共鸣,共振) which dramatically increases systemic vibration.

Part Ⅱ Topics

1. Do you know something about the main engine?

Here is a main engine and a lot of auxiliary machines in the engine room. The main engine is the most important equipment on board. It usually consists of cylinders, pistons, crankshafts, main bearings, connecting rods, cooling system, starting system, lubricating system and operating system. According to the numbers of strokes, the marine engine can be divided into two kinds: 2-stroke and 4-stroke diesel engines.

2. Talk about the dock repair

Normally for class dock survey（2.5 years interval）or if a ship met with a storm during the last voyage and damaged something under water, she has to be dry-docked for inspection and repair. Before going into the dock, the chief engineer will inform the shipyard to send an oil barge for the oil tanks drained and he will also make everything clear about the shore power, cooling water supply and know about the rules of the dock, otherwise the ship will be in the danger of being fined. The dock repair usually includes tail-shaft repair, propeller repair, sea water suction repair, thrust bearing repair and so on.

为了准备面试,新船员尤其要注意的是,不仅要有良好的英语水平,还要能够有熟练的专业知识,只有两者都兼顾了,在面试的过程中才能够结合面试者提出的问题,有效的组织语言,顺利的通过面试。

Chapter 3　Knowledge about Various Kinds of Ships

第 3 章　不同种类船舶的有关知识

Tips

了解各种类型的船舶是每位航海者必备的知识,尤其是即将毕业的学生。在面试前,熟悉船舶类型,有助于找出更适合自己的就业方向。

3.1　杂货船常见问题 Questions about general cargo ships

Part Ⅰ　Questions

1. What are general cargo ships?

   They can also be called multi-purpose vessels, designed to handle and stow a variety of cargo.

2. Do you know the size of general cargo ships?

   General cargo vessels vary in length between 80 m and 160 m, the latter having a dead-weight of about 20,000 tons.

Part Ⅱ　Topics

1. **What kind of cargo can be carried by general cargo ships**?

   This may include forest products, manufactured goods, heavy

equipment, vehicles, machinery, bagged goods, steel and food products, and containers. They can range from canned food(罐装食品), sawn timber(锯木), steel bars (钢条), grain sacks(袋装粮食), manufactured consumer goods packed in cardboard boxes(硬纸板箱), to liquid cargo and vegetable oils.

2. What are the advantages of general cargo ships?

Generally speaking, there are five advantages. Firstly, low tonnage and shallow draft lead to high maneuverability(高机动性); Secondly, convenient cargo handling for its self-contained lifting equipment; Thirdly, being equipped with large hatch covers designed to bear heavy loads and low manufacture as well as operating cost. Besides, for the seaman working on such a ship, it is quite good life, if he can ignore the mess all around. Normally the ship's stay in port will be quite long. This means more leisure time on shore.

General cargo ship

3.2　散货船常见问题 Questions about bulk cargo ships

Part I　Questions

1. What are bulk carriers?

Bulk carriers, or bulk freighters, are merchant ships specially designed to transport unpackaged cargo in its cargo holds.

2. What cargo does bulk carriers carry?

Their cargo can be grains, coal, ore(矿石), sands, fertilizers (肥料), livestock(牲畜) and cement, etc.

3. Do you know about VLBC?

Yes. VLBC refers to Very Large Bulk Carrier.(超大型散货船，约30万吨)

VLBC

Part II　Topics

1. Do you know any abbreviations about bulk carriers?

A number of abbreviations are used to describe bulk carriers.

"OBO" describes a bulk carrier which carries a combination of ore, bulk, and oil, and "O/O" is used for combination oil and ore carriers. The terms "VLOC," "VLBC," "ULOC," and "ULBC" for very large and ultra large ore and bulk carriers were adapted from the supertanker designations very large crude carrier and ultra large crude carrier.

2. What are the types of bulk carriers?

According to the types of cargo, bulk carriers can be divided into coal carriers, timber carriers, ore carriers, cattle ships, grain carriers, etc. When it comes to sizes, bulk carriers can be segregated into six major sizes: small, handysize, handymax, panamax, capesize, and very large.

Commonly used phrases

OBO 石油散货矿砂混装船

O/O 石油散货船

VLOC 超大型矿砂船

VLBC 超大型散货船

ULOC 超巨型矿砂船

ULBC 超巨型散货船

3. 3　集装箱船常见问题 Questions about container ships

Part Ⅰ　Questions

1. What are containers?

Containers are large containers which are used to carry goods across the ocean.

2. What are the types of container ships?

There are three common types of container ship. The "box ship"; the Roll On/Roll Off(RO/RO)ship(滚装船)and Lift On/Lift Off(LO/LO)ship(吊装船).

3. What are the advantages of container ships?

Container ships generally have three advantages: saving manpower and cost in cargo handling; reducing damage to cargo and improving the efficiency of goods circulation.

4. How to measure the loading capacity of container ships?

Container ships are mainly measured in Twenty-foot Equivalent Units(TEU)(20 英尺集装箱), or Forty-foot Equivalent Units (FEU)(40 英尺集装箱). So far today's largest container ship, The Emma MAERSK, has a capacity of about 15,200 TEU.

注:从事集装箱运输的公司有 COSCO(中远), SINOTRANS (外运), China Shipping(中海), MAERSK(马士基)等。

Container

Part Ⅱ   Topics

1. What are the types of containers?

There are a number of container styles, ranging from the basic dry bulk container to the refrigerated container, also known as a reefer(冷藏集装箱). Besides are the Tank Container, Bulk Container,

Platform Based Container, Platform Container, Open Top Container, Car Container, Pen Container or Live Stock Container and Garment Container.

2. What are container ships?

Container ships (or " box ships") carry their cargo packed into standard 20' or 40' containers that are stacked both on and below deck. Smaller "feeder" ships carry containers on coastal and inland waters.

Commonly used phrases

FCL：Full Container Load 整柜

LCL：Less Than Container Load 拼箱

40 HC：40' High Cubic 40 高柜

40' High Refrigerator 40 高冻柜

G. C：General Cargo 普通柜

S. H：Semi Hazardous 半危险品

H. Z：Hazardous 危险品

O/T：Open Top 开顶柜

F/R：Flat rack 框架箱

R. F：Refrigerator 冻柜

CY：Container Yard 集装箱堆场

CFS：Container Freight Station 集装箱货运站

TEU：Twenty-feet Equivalent Units 20 英尺集装箱

FEU：Forty-feet Equivalent Units 40 英尺集装箱

multi-modal transport 多式联运

3.4 油轮常见问题 Questions about oil tankers

Part I Questions

1. What are tankers?

Tankers are designed to transport liquids in bulk. Tankers include oil tankers, the chemical tankers, and the liquefied gas carriers (LPG & LNG).

2. What are oil tankers?

Oil tankers, also known as petroleum tankers, are merchant ships designed for the bulk transport of oil. There are two basic types of oil tankers: the crude tanker and the product tanker.

3. What are crude tankers and product tankers?

Crude tankers move large quantities of unrefined crude oil from its point of extraction to refineries. Product tankers, generally much smaller, are designed to move petrochemicals(石油化学品) from refineries to points near consuming markets.

4. What are VLCC and ULCC?

Both of them are crude oil carriers. VLCC stands for Very Large Crude Oil Carrier whose DWT(dead weight tonnage) is between 200,000 gt to 300,000 gt. ULCC stands for Ultra Large Crude oil Carrier whose DWT is above 300,000 gt.

5. What is IGS(inert gas system)?

According to SOLAS, oil tankers should be provided with an IGS, whose function is to lower the oxygen content inside oil tanks thus avoiding explosion.

6. What is the maximum oxygen content for IGS(惰性气体系统)?

Inert gas system delivers air with an oxygen concentration of less than 5% by volume(Usually less than 5% oxygen).

7. When should oil tanks be inerted?

During cargo discharging and COW(crude oil washing).

8. What is COW?

COW stands for crude oil washing. It means washing out the residue from the tanks of an oil tanker using the original oil cargo itself, after the cargo tanks have been emptied.

9. What kinds of oil tankers should be provided with a COW system?

According to MARPOL73/78, Crude oil washing system becomes mandatory for new tankers of 20,000 tons or more deadweight.

10. Do you know CBT or SBT?

Yes, I know. CBT stands for clean ballast tanks, and SBT means segregated ballast tanks. The purpose of setting them is to reduce oil content in ballast water thus preventing pollution by ships.

11. What do you think a tanker seafarer should pay utmost attention to?

I think he should be of high responsibility to avoid fire accidents and pollution.

12. What special certificate do you hold before working on an oil tanker?

I hold the certificates for the "Special Training on Oil Tanker Familiarization", "Special Training on Oil Tanker Operation" and "Special Training on IGS and COW of Oil Tanker".

Part II   Topics

What are the advantages and disadvantages of COW?

COW has many advantages such as increasing total quantity of cargo oil discharged; reducing corrosion of tank steel; minimum oil pollution by reducing oil content in washing water and reducing sea water in cargo oil. However, COW also has some shortcomings like prolonged discharging time and increased workload.

Commonly used phrases and background knowledge

inert 惰性的

DWT: dead weight tonnage 载重吨

VLCC: Very Large Crude oil Carrier 超级油轮

ULCC: Ultra Large Crude oil Carrier 巨型油轮

IGS：inert gas system 惰性气体系统

COW：crude oil washing system 原油洗舱系统

SBT：segregated ballast tank 专用压载舱

CBT：clean ballast tank 清洁压载舱

Special Training On Oil Tanker Familiarization 油轮安全知识特殊培训

Special Training On Oil Tanker Operation 油轮安全操作特殊培训

Special Training On IGS and COW of Oil Tanker 惰性气体和原油洗舱培训

Oil tanker

世界造船业将油轮按载重吨位分为 5 个级别：①巴拿马型（Panamax）：船型以巴拿马运河（Panama Canal）通航条件为上限（譬如运河对船宽、吃水的限制），载重吨（DWT）在 6～8 万吨之间。②阿芙拉型（Aframax）：平均运费指数 AFRA（Average Freight Rate Assessment）最高船型，经济性最佳，是适合白令海（Bering Sea）冰区航行油船的最佳船型。载重吨在 8～12 万吨之间。③苏伊士型(Suezmax):船型以苏伊士运河(Suez Canal)通航条件为上限,载重吨在 12～20 万吨之间。④VLCC(Very Large Crude oil Carrier):巨型原油船,载重吨在 20～30 万吨之间。⑤ULCC(Ultra Large Crude oil Carrier):超巨型原油船,载重吨在 30 万吨以上。

3.5 散装化学品、液体船常见问题 Questions about chemical carriers and liquid cargo ships

Part I Questions

1. What are chemical tankers?

   Chemical tankers are tankers designed to transport chemicals in bulk. And normally these chemicals are of corrosive, toxic, flammable and volatile(挥发的)action.

2. How many types of chemical tankers do you know?

   Three types. According to their purposes, chemical tankers can be divided into specialized chemical tanker, parcel chemical tanker and chemical/product tanker.

3. Have you heard about Liquefied gas carriers?

   Yes, I know them. Liquefied Gas carriers are specialized vessels that are used to transport Liquefied Natural Gas (LNG) and Liquefied Petroleum Gas(LPG) under controlled temperature and pressure.

4. What qualities do you think a seafarer on chemical tanker should have?

   In my opinion, if a seafarer is sent to a chemical tanker, he should be responsible, cautious and always put safety in the first place to avoid any accidents.

5. What special certificates do you hold before working on a chemical tanker?

I hold the certificates for "Special Training on Chemical Tanker Familiarization" and "Special Training on Chemical Tanker Operation".

Part II　Topics

What do you know about liquefied natural gas(LNG) and liquefied petroleum gas(LPG)?

Liquefied natural gas means the natural gas that has been liquefied by reducing its temperature to −162 ℃ at atmospheric pressure. In this way, the space requirements for storage and transport are reduced. The latter refers to propane(丙烷), butane(丁烷) and their isomer (同分异构物) gases at atmospheric pressure(大气压力) and normal temperature.

Commonly used phrases

LNG：Liquefied Natural Gas 液化天然气

LPG：Liquefied Petroleum Gas 液化石油气

specialized chemical tanker 专用化学品船

parcel chemical tanker 多功能化学品船

chemical/product tanker 兼用化学品船

化学品船安全知识特殊培训（Special Training on Chemical Tanker Familiarization）

化学品船安全操作特殊培训（Special Training on Chemical Tanker Operation）

Chemical carrier

LNG carrier

Chapter 4　Test of International Maritime Laws and Regulations

第4章　海事法规的测试

4.1　港口国检查 PSC Inspection

Tips

港口国检查(Port State Control)是港口当局对到港的外国船舶依法实施的以船舶技术状况、操作性要求、船舶配员、船员生活和工作条件为检查对象的,以确保船舶和人命财产安全、防止海洋污染为宗旨的一种监督与控制,是有效限制低标准船舶在海上营运的有力措施。作为船上高级船

PSC inspection in the engine room

员,应熟悉 PSC 检查的程序,基于的国际公约,检查的文件和证书,详细检查的明显证据,滞留,优先检查和扩大检查等,了解"巴黎备忘录(Paris MOU)"、"东京备忘录(Tokyo MOU)"等 PSC 组织的港口国监督体系。关于港口国检查常见问题有:①什么是

PSC？全称是什么？②PSC 主要检查什么？哪些缺陷可能使检查官进行更详细的检查？哪些缺陷可能导致船舶被滞留？

Part I Questions

1. What is the purpose of the PSC inspection?

   The purpose for PSC inspection is to ensure safety of life and the pollution prevention at sea.

2. What equipment does PSCO usually check in the PSC inspection?

   Usually they pay more attention to the safety equipment, fire fighting equipment, life saving equipment, emergency equipment and pollution prevention equipment and so on.

3. What device does PSCO pay most attention to?

   The PSCO will pay most attention to the emergency equipment and the pollution prevention equipment on board.

   注:检查官特别注重关键性设备,如应急设备,消防安全设备,救生设备等。

4. What kind of deficiencies will be seen the most serious?

   The fire-fighting equipment, pollution prevention equipment and life-saving equipment, any of them if found in trouble, can be seen as the most serious.

5. What is your working language on board your ship?

   The crewmembers in our engine department usually use Chinese to communicate with each other, but our senior engineers can communicate with others in English. So language problem will not affect our daily work at all.

   注:如果你们的船员来自各个国家,你也可以这样回答:We are from different countries, like Malaysia, India, Singapore or Russia, so English is our working language. If we cannot communicate with each other, the orders and instructions can not be understood, and this may cause major accidents.

6. What will happen when the PSCO finds that emergency fire pump fails to work?

The ship will be detained or delayed.

7. What would happen if your ship were found serious deficiencies during the PSC inspection?

The ship may be delayed or detained.

8. What is the near accident? Please give an example to show your understanding.

The near accident is a kind of potential danger. If it is worse, it will become an accident. For example, two ships are in close quarters situation.

9. What is clear ground?

It is an evidence that a deficiency or severe deficiencies have been inspected. For example, invalid certificates, serious structural deficiencies, fire prevention deficiencies and so on.

10. In addition to Paris MOU, what are the other MOUs?

Latin-American MOU, Tokyo MOU, Indian Ocean MOU, Caribbean MOU, Abuja MOU, Mediterranean MOU and so on. USCG is an independent one.

11. How do you receive PSCO?

Prepare a rest room and all the certificates and documents. One officer should be chosen to accompany PSCO. If a deficiency has been found, immediately contact the captain and consult with PSCO to find a possible approach to eliminate or diminish the deficiency. The first impression given to the PSCO is very important.

12. How many measures are there for a PSCO to rectify the deficiency?

For example rectify before sailing, rectify within 14 days, rectify before arrival at next port, rectify within 3 months, detain the ship, inform the flag state, etc.

Part Ⅱ Topics

1. What is PSC?

PSC means the Port State Control. It is based on some international conventions like SOLAS, STCW, LOAD LINE 66, ITC 69, MARPOL Convention. The PSCO will inspect some certificates and documents: IOPP, Oil Record Book, Minimum Safe Manning Certificate, SOPEP, Fire Control Plan, previous survey report file, Medical Certificate, Certificate of Competency. Some equipment in the engine room should be inspected, such as main engine, boiler, generator, emergency equipment, fire fighting equipment, anti-pollution equipment, life saving apparatus and so on. If deficiencies are found, the PSCO will report it to the port authority and ask us to rectify them at once or before we reach our next port of call. If serious deficiencies are found, our ship will be detained.

2. Say something about your experience about PSC inspection

Last voyage in USA, I experienced the PSC inspection. The PSCO inspected our engine room, asked us to operate the oil water separator, incinerator. He checked the Oil Record Book. There was one deficiency in our department. There was no auto-shut down device installed on the oil water separator according to the IOPP requirements. So the PSCO asked us to rectify it immediately.

注:机舱部检查常见的缺陷:油水分离器15ppm报警器缺陷;分油机间残油过多;机舱油水的标准排放接头应有明显的标记,原来标记为:BILGE WATERS,要求改为:ENGINE ROOM BILGES TO SHORE RECEPTION;卫生水排放接头应标记为:SOIL TO SHORE RECEPTION(新加坡要求),舵机舵角指示和驾驶台的指示不能相差一度;舵机及舵机间不清洁干净;舵机失电时,驾驶台没有报警;舵机间堆放液压油,舵机推力杆油封漏油,底部积油太多;舵机系统油漏泄;舵机间存放易燃物品;舵机房多余的消防员备品箱没移走;舵机房机械通风装置需修理;舵机液压管漏油;机

舱大通风筒自动关闭开关不太灵活;机舱烟筒顶的防水板开关,船员不熟悉;应急发电机间发电机风冷出口挡板不活络;伙房通风打开不灵便;机舱风筒自闭装置不活络;烟筒百叶窗关闭不严;机舱风筒开关方向标反;机舱门和舵机房门自动关闭功能失常;机舱烟筒及通风筒锈穿有洞;机舱一些防火门自动关闭装置失效;甲板通往烟囱的栈道有洞;机舱通风筒挡板气缸漏气等。

3. As a chief engineer, talk about your responsibility for PSC inspection.

As a chief engineer, he should check all the equipment and systems, especially the fire fighting equipment, the life saving equipment, the emergency equipment, the escape routes from the machinery space and prepare some documents in the engine department, like Oil Record Book, the IOPP certificate, and so on. Also he should ask the crew to clean the engine room and equipment. Ask someone to receive the PSC and accompany him. He should also cooperate with other departments to make everything ready for the PSC inspection.

Commonly used phrases

Port State Control 港口国监督

competency 资格;能力(等于 competence)

entitle 使……有权利

target *n.* 目标;靶子 *v.* 把……作为目标

database 数据库,资料库

detention 挽留;延迟

weathertight 防风雨的

clear grounds(obvious evidence) 明显证据

International Tonnage Measurement 1969(ITC69) 国际船舶吨位丈量公约

4.2 国际防止船舶污染公约 MARPOL

Tips

一直以来,海洋环境污染比较严重,大大影响了人类和海洋生物的安全和存在。为了保护环境,IMO 多次制订、修改和补充了 MARPOL78/95 公约。目前有 6 个附则。船员应了解 MARPOL 公约的历史,6 个附则的主要内容及生效日期。学员们可重点关注防止油污染,大气污染,垃圾污染方面的规定。面试问题包括:①MARPOL 公约有几个附则? 生效的附则有哪些? ②现行有效的防污染规则是什么? ③什么是 IOPP 证书? 有效期是多少? ④何谓 15 ppm? 机舱有哪些防污染设备? 机舱污水怎样排放? 油渣怎样处理? ⑤什么是 SOPEP? 加装燃油时应注意什么? ⑥怎样制定垃圾管理计划? 怎样处理塑料垃圾?

Part I Questions

1. What do you know about MARPOL?

   MARPOL Convention stands for International Convention on Pollution Prevention from Ships, it is to prevent pollution at sea from ships. It has 6 Annexes.

2. How do you deal with the ash remaining in the incinerator?

   At first store them in the covered metal drums, after getting alongside the port, they will be sent ashore.

3. What language do you use in your Oil Record Book?

   We insist to use dual languages, Chinese and English, to write down anything in the Oil Record Book.

   注:油类记录簿应该用英语或法语书写。中国籍船上是用中文写的。

4. How many sludge tanks do you have and tell me their capacity altogether?

We have two sludge tanks and the total capacity is 30 m³ (cubic meters).

注:具体按照实际回答。

5. How do you dispose of the oily waste?

   Oil sludge and oily rags are burnt out in an incinerator and oily bilge is separated by oily water separators. If possible, discharge them ashore.

6. How many tons of oily waste can be burnt by your incinerator per hour?

   About 50 kgs per hour.

7. If the incinerator is out of order, what will you do then?

   Usually we store oil sludge in the sludge tank and put oily rags into the covered metal drums. And then find out the trouble of the incinerator.

8. How much fuel oil have you consumed everyday/in the voyage?

   About 20 ~ 25 tons every/per day. It depends upon the days we spent in the whole voyage.

9. What does ODMS refer to?

   It refers to oil discharge monitor system.

10. Have you ever seen SOPEP? What is SOPEP?

    Yes, of course. SOPEP stands for Shipboard Oil Pollution Emergency Plan.

11. Can you tell me some oil pollution prevention equipment?

    Oily water separator, incinerator, and sewage treatment plant.

12. How do you handle the oily wastes on board?

    Oily wastes should be put into the covered metal drums and burnt in the incinerator at regular intervals or sent ashore if possible.

13. What is the function of the incinerator?

    Incinerator is used to burn out oily rags and sludge.

14. What are the Annexes of MARPOL?

Annex Ⅰ: Regulation for the prevention of pollution by oil

Annex Ⅱ: Regulation for control of pollution by noxious liquid substances in bulk

Annex Ⅲ: Regulation for the prevention of pollution by harmful substances carried by sea in packaged form

Annex Ⅳ: Regulation for prevention of pollution by sewage

Annex Ⅴ: Regulation for prevention of pollution by garbage from ship

Annex Ⅵ: Regulation for prevention of pollution by exhaust from ship

15. What is IOPP? What is the valid period?

International Oil Pollution Prevention Certificate, it is valid for 5 years.

16. Which operation should be entered into the Oil Record Book Part Ⅰ, internal transfer of fuel oil or disposal of oil residues?

Disposal of oil residues.

17. What kind of ships should be provided with Oil Record Book Part Ⅰ?

Ships of 150 tons gross tonnage and above and all ships of 400 tons gross tonnage and above, other than oil tankers.

18. Which equipment must be used when discharging the bilge water overboard?

Oil water separator.

19. What is an Oil Record Book?

The Oil Record Book is used to keep records of all the operations of oil and disposal of oil sludge, bilge water, cargo/ballast operation for oil pollution prevention.

20. What does ORB stand for?

Oil Record Book.

21. How can an oily water separator separate water and oil?

The operating principle is to use the difference of density of oil and water. The oily water mixture first goes to the coarse separating compartment, here some oil is separated because of low density and rises into the oil collection space. And then the remaining mixture goes to the fine separating compartment and more oil is separated, then the remaining mixture goes to the two-stage filters to remove oil.

22. Who is in charge of the oily water separator on board ship?

The fourth engineer.

23. If you see oil/grease stains in the engine room. What will you do?

I will remove it immediately and check the causes. If it is out of reach, I will report it at once.

24. What operations are recorded in the Oil Record Book Part Ⅰ? Can you list some items?

Machinery space operations. Any operation concerning oil or oily waste should be entered in the Oil Record Book, like discharging bilge water, disposal of oil residues, ballasting of fuel tanks and so on.

25. If you find your vessel leaks out oil, what measures will you take?

Give alarm, prepare some materials to deal with it/Take action according to SOPEP.

26. Can you discharge bilge water overboard directly? What equipment should you use? How do you deal with bilges?

Absolutely no. We must use some equipment like oil water separator to deal with bilges.

27. What is the requirement of oil content pumped out overboard?

Oil content in the oil should be less than 15 PPM.

28. What garbage can be discharged into the sea within Special Area?

   Food waste comminuted.

29. The Garbage Record Book, as a part of the ship's official logbook. How long shall it be kept on board and preserved?

   2 years after the last entry.

30. What is the distance limit when oily waste from cargo tanks of oil tankers can be discharged?

   50 nautical miles away from the nearest land.

31. When did MARPOL Convention come into force?

   Oct. 2, 1983.

32. What prevention should you take before bunkering?

   We will make out the bunkering plan, arrange someone to plug the deck scuppers firmly, ask someone to keep watch at the bunkering station and ship's sides. Prepare some anti-pollution materials, like rags, sawdust, oil boom and bucket.

33. What should you pay attention to when the tank is nearly full during bunkering?

   We will take sounding frequently and reduce the pumping speed when the tank is nearly full.

34. After bunkering, what pollution prevention actions will you take?

   We will flush the hose with compressed air and remove the oil remaining in the hose in a container.

35. Can we discharge plastics into the sea at will?

   No, we can not discharge it into the sea anywhere.

36. What garbage can be discharged within the special area?

   The victual waste (food waste) ground, but it should be more than 12 miles from the nearest land.

   注:粉碎成粉的食品废物能在特殊区域内排放,但要离最近的陆地12海里。

37. How often should the SOPEP gear (Oil Spill Equipment) be tested? Who tests it?

The chief officer or the chief engineer tests it monthly.

38. How often is the sewage plant operation tested? Who tests it?

The second engineer tests it prior to discharge monthly.

39. How often do you carry out an oil spill drill?

It depends on the company's regulations. Usually once three months.

40. How often do you have a SOPEP drill?

It depends on the company's regulations. Usually once three months. We can refer to regulations of SOPEP equipped on board ship.

41. If you found an oil spill in the sea, how would you react?

According to SOPEP, immediately report to the nearest competent port authority and take positive action to control the pollution like using oil boom and make an entry in the logbook.

Part Ⅱ　Topics

1. How do you prevent pollution to the sea on board ship?

There are some types of pollution to the sea caused by oil, noxious liquid substance, harmful substance, sewage, garbage and exhaust gas. In order to prevent pollution and comply with MARPOL Convention, we have to use anti-pollution equipment including incinerator, oil water separator, slop tank, sludge and sewage tanks, and sewage treatment tank. The general method of pollution prevention is to use oil water separator to treat bilge water, burn out the sludge and wastes in the incinerator, store the oily rags, sludge and oily wastes in the different color bins. Sewage treatment plant is used to treat sewage water. Also, we can discharge them to the shore reception facilities when we call at the port.

2. Talk about the entries of the Oil Record Book

The Oil Record Book Part I shall be provided to every oil tanker of 150 tons gross tonnage and above and every ship of 400 tons gross tonnage and above, other than the oil tanker to record machinery space operations, such as the disposal of oil residues and sludge, the automatic and non-automatic discharge of bilge water, the accidental and exceptional failure of the pollution prevention equipment, etc. Oil Record Book Part II is to provide every oil tanker to record relevant cargo/ballast operation. When making entries, the date, operational code and item number shall be inserted in the appropriate columns and the required particulars shall be recorded in the blank spaces and it must be written in English or French.

3. Talk about the treatments of dirty wastes and rags, especially plastic wastes on board your ship

MARPOL Convention provides for detailed regulations on garbage disposal. Every shipping company has its own Garbage Management Plan in its ISM documents and the chief engineer or the chief officer is the designated person in charge of carrying out the garbage disposal, but all crew on board should follow the garbage management plan.

According to the plan, all dirty wastes and rags will be collected and put into garbage bins of different colors, some are burned out in the incinerator. Plastics must be put into the red bin and can not be burned in the incinerator or discharge it into the sea. When reaching a certain amount, it can be transferred to the shore reception facilities.

Commonly used phrases

instantaneous discharging rate 瞬时排放率

slop tank 污水柜

oil boom 油围栏

shore reception facilities 岸上接收设施

stringent requirement 严厉的要求

ban *v.* 禁止,取缔 *n.* 禁令,禁忌

compactor 垃圾捣碎机

comminuter 粉碎机

dunnage 垫舱物料

International Oil Pollution Prevention Certificates(IOPP) 国际防止油污证书

Shipboard Oil Pollution Emergency Plan(SOPEP) 船舶油污应急计划

Shipboard Marine Pollution Emergency Plan(SMPEP) 船舶海洋污染应急计划

4.3 国际海上人命安全公约 SOLAS Convention

Tips

国际海上人命安全公约 SOLAS 是和安全最有关的国际公约,规定了适合安全的船舶结构、设备和操作最低标准。我们应接受海难事故的教训,严格按照 SOLAS 公约中有关消防、救生设备和演练,弃船演习,通信设备和电气设备的维护与使用,ISPS 规则等的规定,以确保船舶、货物、环境、个人和同船船员的安全,认真执行公司的安全管理体系(SMS)。学员要熟悉 SOLAS 公约精神。

Part I Questions

1. What is SOLAS?

   The International Convention for the Safety of Life at Sea(SOLAS) is an international maritime safety treaty.

2. What is special for the 1974 version of SOLAS?

   The 1974 version includes the tacit acceptance procedure(默认接受程序).

3. What is the aim of SOLAS Convention?

To prevent pollution at sea, ensure the safety of ships and promote shipping trade.

4. According to SOLAS, what safety measures should be carried out by Company?

Establish SMS according to ISM and designate a person or persons ashore.

5. How do you mark the escape route in the engine room?

The escape route has been marked in arrows and these arrows can be clearly sighted in dark.

6. How often do you perform a fire fighting drill? Who controls on the spot?

Once a month. In the engine department, the chief engineer will control on the spot.

7. How often do you have a boat drill or fire drill?

Once a month.

8. How often should the emergency generator be started?

Usually once a week.

9. How often should the emergency fire pump be started?

Once a week.

10. What are the critical operations and conditions?

Critical operations and conditions are those which have a significant risk of causing major injuries or illness to people, or damage to ship, cargo, other property and/or the environment.

Part II Topics

1. Talk about a fire and boat drill

As required, we should carry out the fire drill and boat drill once every month. The chief engineer and chief officer should be in charge of the fire drill and life boat drill. During the drills we use some fire fighting equipment and life-saving apparatus. So we should always keep them in good order. The equipment used in the drills includes the life boat, life jacket, fire pumps, fire fighting apparatus and so on. All the crew members in the engine department will take part in it.

2. Talk about the fire prevention and fire fighting on board ship

Fire on board is a serious threat to the safety to ship and crew. So we have to take every precaution to prevent fire on board, for example, keep good housekeeping and putting different wastes in the different color bins, keep fuel away from heat, get "permit-to-work" before carrying out welding work, and so on. The fire fighting apparatus are fire hydrant, fire hose, portable extinguisher and fixed installation. The general methods are smothering mode, the isolating mode, the cooling mode, and the chemical inhibiting mode.

3. Do you know abandoning ship procedures? Name the procedures.

First sound the alarm. All persons with lifejackets mustered at the assembly station. Roll call will be executed. Ask the duties and knowledge of life drills. Embark in the lifeboat. Prepare to launch the lifeboat. Test communication equipment, navigation equipment and machineries. Launch liferafts. Lower boats to the surface of the water and start lifeboat engine clear of the mother vessel. Rig in and secure the lifeboat. Assess the performance of personnel by ship master or person in charge of the life drill.

注:有些船公司把点名的环节放在最后,但是大同小异。

Commonly used phrases

amendment (法律、文件的)改动,修正案

treaty 条约,协议

tacit acceptance 默认程序

in breach of 违反

comply with/in compliance with 遵守,符合

4.4 国际安全管理规则 ISM Code

Tips

ISM 规则是 SOLAS 公约新增的第 IX 章内容的一部分,是 1998 年 7 月 1 日生效的强制性规则,要求船公司及其船舶必须建立安全管理体系,建立全球性的安全管理监控机制,以保证船舶安全营运和防止海洋污染,最大限度地控制海难事故的发生。船舶应按照 SMS 有关规定严格执行。ISM 规则在各港口国检查中都被作为重点,是船东面试的一个重要内容。因此,要求船长、轮机长、驾驶员和轮机员都要熟练掌握 ISM 规则的内容,以及在本公司实施情况及安全管理体系运转情况等。

关于 ISM 规则常见问题有:①ISM 规则是什么? 目标是什么? 主要内容是什么? ②ISM 规则生效后船上多了哪些证书? DOC 与 SMC 全称是什么? ③船上发现不符合情况或需要岸基支持时,船长应向谁报告? ④DPA 是什么意思? 全称是什么?

Part I Questions

1. What do you know about ISM?

   It stands for International Safety Management. It was adopted by IMO in 1994. Now it is attached to Chapter Nine of the SOLAS Convention.

2. What are the contents of ISM code? /What do you know about ISM code?

   The ISM code includes the following contents:

   Terms and definitions, objectives, safety and environmental protection policy, company responsibilities and authority, designated persons, master's responsibility and authority, resources and personnel, development of plans for shipboard operations, emergency preparedness, reports and analysis of non-conformities, accidents and hazardous occurrences, maintenance of the ship and equipment, documentation, company verification, review and evaluation, certification and verification.

3. What kind of ships is the ISM Code applicable to?

All ships.

4. What are the objectives of ISM Code?

Ensure safety of ship at sea, avoid loss or injury to people, prevent the damage to the environment, especially to the marine environment.

5. What's the meaning of designated person in SMS?

He is a person ashore who has direct access to the highest level of management. His responsibility and authority include monitoring the safety and pollution-prevention of each ship.

注:DPA 岸方指定人员。职责是代表船东负责防污染,安全操作方面的事务。

6. What is a safety meeting?

Safety meeting can be called SEP meeting, held by the Shipboard Safety Committee. Its main purpose is to ensure safe operations of the ship and protection of marine environment. The intervals of the meeting can not exceed one month.

7. How often do you have a safety meeting?

According to the SMS on my last board, it is one-month interval.

8. What are the other people to attend the meeting concerning safety?

For a department meeting, all personnel except for duty officer and ratings in this department must attend the meeting. In addition, Captain and senior officers also have another safety meetings.

9. What does DOC imply?

Document of Compliance. 符合文件

注:每个航运公司都应建立维护程序去控制所有与 SMS 有关的文件和数据。每条船都应该携带与本船有关的所有文件。

10. What is SMC?

SMC stands for Safety Management Certificate.

注:SMC 是安全管理证书。它是由船旗国指定的机构和组织对船舶签署的证书。

11. What is NCR in ISM Code?

Non-conformity Report.

注:不符合报告。重大不符合指:Major non-conformity is an identifiable deviation which poses a serious threat to personnel or ship safety or serious risk to environment. It requires immediate correction action.

12. When some new rules or acts referred to your department need to be studied, who will arrange it?

Chief engineer.

13. What is the critical equipment and system?

Main engine, emergency equipment, generators, windlass, steering gear, emergency fire pump, auxiliary boiler, cooling water system, fuel transfer system, lubrication system—those that are very important for the ship's operation, failing of which will cause a serious trouble or accident.

14. What are the critical operations and conditions?

Critical operations and conditions are those which have a significant risk of causing major injuries or illness to people, or damage to ship, cargo, other property and/or the environment.

注:关键操作及临界状况指能够引起对人员造成重大伤害,造成船舶损坏,货物或其他的财产和环境的损坏的重大危险的操作。

15. What is the near accident? Please give an example to show your understanding.

The near accident is a kind of potential danger. If it is worse, it will become an accident. For example, two ships are in close quarters situation.

16. What is the purpose of ISM audit?

Audit is the systematic and independent verification to determine whether ISM activities and results conform to planned arrangements and whether these arrangements are effectively performed to achieve the objectives of the company and relevant maritime laws.

注:审核是系统且不受约束地去检查 ISM 活动和结果是否符合计划的安排,是否这些安排是预先有效地达到公司和海事法规的目标。

17. The ISM Code requires preventive maintenance schedules. How do you make your maintenance schedules?

According to ISM Code, the preventive maintenance plan is made based on the ship's "Planned Maintenance System" and the machinery running hours records. This plan should be made on an annual basis (for a five-year basis). Usually, the monthly maintenance schedules are made based on the annual preventive maintenance plan and the basic occasional maintenance work.

注:大管轮负责 PMS。

18. What enforcement action would be taken on the vessels without being in compliance with ISM Code?

The results of the audit will be brought to the attention of the relevant persons, and they should take positive action to remedy these non-conformities.

19. What key elements does a Safety Management System include?

(1) Safety and environmental protection policy.

(2) Instructions and procedures to ensure safety operations and environmental protection in compliance with relevant international and flag state legislation.

(3) Defined levels of authority and lines of communication between shore and shipboard personnel.

(4) Procedures for reporting accidents and non-conformities with the SMS and the Code.

(5) Procedures to prepare for and respond to emergencies.

(6) Procedures for internal audits and management reviews.

20. Where would you expect to find the Company's various SMS Manuals?

In the Captain's and C/E's cabins.

21. What are the internal audit and external audit?

Internal audit is carried out by DPA, Superintendent, safety master, or even manager from the shipping company. Every ship is compulsory to receive inspection created by an internal audit within a year. The external audit is carried out by the Administration or its authorized organization, such as the classification society.

22. If the chief engineer were not on board, who would assume his responsibilities?

According to SMS and common practice, the second engineer will take over the responsibilities.

23. Who will complete the Appraisal Form for the engine department personnel?

The chief engineer will fulfill in that form and submit it to the shipmaster.

注:一般由轮机长为轮机部人员作鉴定。

24. Have you been involved in any ship casualty, including pollution incident?

No, I haven't. I always keep pollution prevention in mind.

25. How do you ensure that the Company's policies are implemented on board?

The company should establish some procedures to make everyone know about the company's procedures, make clear everyone's responsibilities and authorities and implement the company's policies. Someone is designated to supervise the implementation.

26. What is Internal Audit and External?

Usually once a year to carry out internal audit and the relevant documents and records will be checked. the auditor will check machines and maintenance standards on the spot. If there are any deficiencies, we should rectify them and report the actions already taken to the auditor. Usually once every three years to carry out the external audit by the recognized authorities.

27. Have you participated in any Audit before? If so, give a brief account, including the results of the Audit.

Yes. There were some deficiencies, like the recording was not complete. No records for the drills. Or sometimes the ORB was falsely recorded.

28. What is the right procedure to correct an erroneous entry in any log book, checklist, work book, record book, etc.?

Cross a line on the wrong entry, making it still clear and initiate the right one at the side.

29. Why is "reporting" necessary?

If you are unsure of the action to take or the situation is very serious or urgent, you should report it to avoid accidents.

Part II   Topics

1. Say something about ISM Code and the maintenance of ISM Code

Everybody should study the ISM Code and know about the SMS regulations and have a meeting regularly. We should have an internal audit and external audit regularly, try to comply with the SMS. In the SMS, everybody's duties and responsibilities should be made clear and documented in the SMS. There should be a DPA to monitor the safety of each ship and provide necessary shore-based support.

2. As a chief engineer, talk about your responsibilities according to your company's SMS.

As a chief engineer, I must be responsible to the captain for the whole engine department. It's very important for a chief engineer to be skillful and proficient at work. I should maintain good management and assign jobs fairly among the crew in the engine department. I must also be good at English and language communication and maintain good relationship with captain, the technical superintendent and other personnel from the company, the other engineers and the officer as well.

注:也可这样回答

The C/E is ultimately responsible for the safe and efficient operation of all mechanical and electric equipment. He is responsible for organizing the engine equipment activities in the most cost, effective and safe manner. He is responsible for operative status of the equipment and answers the Captain's advice and alerts the Captain of any possible delays to repair machinery. He is responsible for keeping operational manuals and certificates of his department. He is responsible for training engineering staff to meet the requirements of their jobs and filling the Appraisal Forms.

3. As a second engineer, talk about your responsibilities according to your company's SMS.

As a second engineer, I must work under the leadership of the chief engineer. I should be responsible for the management of the engine department personnel, all maintenance and repair jobs, the main engine and its auxiliary equipment, steering gears, the emergency equipment, requisition for spare parts and stores, supervision of the jobs of engine crew, etc. And I should also keep watch from 0400 to 0800 both in the morning and in the evening except for UMS operation when ship sailing.

注:也可这样回答

The 2nd engineer is responsible for watching period of 0400—0800 in the morning and in the evening when ship sailing. He is responsible to the Chief Engineer for the operation and maintenance of all machinery and associated equipment. He is responsible for deck, electrical, hydraulic and mechanical working conditions. He is responsible for the cleanliness of the engine room and associated compartments. He is responsible for assisting the C/E in the preparation of spare parts and repair list. He is responsible for assuming the C/E's duties if the C/E is absent.

4. As a third engineer, talk about your responsibilities according to your company's SMS.

As a third engineer, the responsibilities include the following: keeping watch from 0000 to 0400 both in the morning and in the evening when ship sailing. Do the maintenance and repair of generator engines, generators, fuel oil purifiers, emergency generator, etc., sound the fuel and lube oil tanks and making records of the daily consumption rate, requisition for spare parts of the machines and equipment under my charge. In general, I should completely accomplish any other duties designated by the chief engineer.

注:也可这样回答

The 3rd engineer is on duty at periods of 0000—0400 in the morning and in the evening when ship sailing. He is responsible for the operation, maintenance and repair of generators, steering gears and auxiliary boilers under the direction of the superior officer. He is responsible for taking measures in safe and efficient operation of all machinery and preventive measures against fire and oil pollution. He is responsible for carrying out the instructions of the deck duty officer related to ballasting and deballasting and record of the operations. He is responsible for maintenance and, overhaul and upkeep of all electrical equipment under the direction of the C/E for preparation of electrical stores and spare parts. He is responsible to the C/E for the monitoring of temperature of vessel's reefer chambers.

5. As a fourth engineer, talk about your responsibilities according to your company's SMS.

I keep watch from 8 to 12 in the morning and in the evening when ship sailing, and during the watch, I should make a round in the E/R, and take readings of all gauges and meters, record the temperatures, esp. the exhaust temperature, and the levels of oil and water, the viscosity of oil and the pressures. I should keep the main engine and some auxiliary machinery and some deck machinery in good order. I should carry out the bridge orders immediately and instructions of the Second Engineer and the Chief Engineer. I should keep the engine room clean and tidy.

注:也可这样回答

The 4th engineer is responsible for watching at periods of 0800—1200 in the morning and in the evening when ship sailing. He is responsible for assisting the 2nd engineer in all technical aspects. He is responsible for operation and maintenance of other auxiliary machinery except that taken by the 3rd engineer. He should take positive measures in the safe and efficient operation of all machinery and guarding against fire and oil pollution. He is responsible for assisting in bunkering and fuel transfer operation under the direction of the 3rd engineer. He is responsible for assisting the 2nd engineer in testing of emergency fire pump and life boat engine.

6. What is SMS?

It stands for safety management system. Shipping company should establish SMS according to ISM code. Anyway, it should include the following functional requirements:

(1) Safety and environmental protection policy.

(2) Instructions and protection of the environment.

(3) Defined levels of authority and lines of communications among shore and shipboard crew.

(4) Procedures for reporting accidents.

(5) Procedures to prepare and react to emergency situations.

(6) Procedures for internal audits and management reviews.

Commonly used phrases

internal audit 内审

external audit 外审

shore-based resources 岸方支援

Planned Maintenance System(PMS) 计划维养体系

4.5　国际船舶和港口设施保安规则 ISPS Code

Tips

船员要熟悉 ISPS 规则目的、对船舶和港口设施的功能性要求、三个安全等级并能说说船上的一些保安措施。

Part Ⅰ　Questions

1. What is ISPS?

International Ship and Port Facility Security

2. What does SSO stand for in the ISPS Code?

Ship Security Officer 船舶保安员

3. What does CSO stand for in the ISPS Code?

Company Security Officer 公司保安员

4. What does SSP stand for in the ISPS Code?

Ship Security Plan 船舶保安计划

5. What does SSA stand for in the ISPS Code?

Ship Security Assessment 船舶保安评估

6. What does DOS stand for in the ISPS Code?

Declaration of Security 保安申明

7. What does SSAS stand for in the ISPS Code?

Ship Security Alert System 船舶保安警报系统

8. What does ISSC stand for in the ISPS Code?

International Ship Security Certificate 国际船舶保安证书

9. What does PFSO stand for in the ISPS Code?

Port & Facility Security Officer 港口设施保安员

10. What does RSO stand for in the ISPS Code?

Recognized Security Organization 认可的保安组织

11. How often do you perform security drills?

At least once every three months.

12. What are the possible crimes if the ship's security is not properly maintained?

The ship is likely to be visited by persons with criminal intent. In addition, the adverse effect on the profitable operation of the ship resulting from theft of cargo or ship's stores, the planning of illegal drugs, the boarding of stowaways and any other unwelcome visitors will occur.

注:criminal intent 犯罪企图;adverse effect 反作用;illegal drugs 毒品;stowaways 偷渡者。

13. What are Security Levels "1, 2 and 3"?

The three levels of security. And they correspond with normal, medium and high threat situations.

14. What is "Restricted area"?

Usually the radio room, chart room and so on.

15. How will you maintain on-board security?

At sea: keep watch and stay alert, switch on search lights in some vulnerable areas, get fire pump ready.

In port: restrict the entry of unfamiliar people, keep watch, search for stowaways and pirates.

Security drill

Part Ⅱ　Topics

What measures do you take to prevent piracy?

Piracy is a headache problem. We should take some measures against piracy. For example, we maintain Security Level 1 at any time. We should control the access to the ship, restrict the flow of information of departure and arrival of ship, fit additional fire hoses, warning sirens and search lights, double the watch, inform the nearest port and authority after the attack and do not risk the safety of crew and passengers.

注:主要保安措施:保持值班警惕,船舶巡逻,防范有外人入船,不透露船舶进出港和路线的消息,如遇到海盗袭击时,要及时与最近的港口和当局联系,不要以船员和乘客的生命冒险。

4.6 国际船员培训、发证和值班标准公约 International Convention on Standards of Training, Certification and Watchkeeping for Seafarers(STCW)

Tips

1978 年采纳 STCW,经历过 1995 年,2010 年大的修改,目的是使公约中的规定适应时代发展,符合船舶安全对于船员培训、发证和值班的最低要求。2010 年马尼拉修正案中提出了新增电子员和电子技工发证和资格的强制性最低要求,现代技术如电子海图显示和信息系统(ECDIS)的要求,应对海盗袭击的新的安全培训要求等。船员们应认真研究 STCW 公约,履行 2010 年 STCW 马尼拉修正案。扩展阅读 STCW 公约有关船长、甲板部、轮机部、无线电通信员、值班、特种船舶、环境保护、防止海盗袭击,驾驶台资源管理和机舱资源管理等具体要求。

Part I Questions

1. What is STCW?

   The STCW Convention stands for the International Convention on Standards of Training, Certification, and Watchkeeping for Seafarers. It was made in 1978, amended in 1995. Now the latest one is Manila Amendments in 2010.

2. What are the levels of crew?

   Three levels: management level, the operational level, support level.

3. How many parts are there for STCW convention?

   Two Parts.

   Part A: mandatory standards regarding provisions of the annex to STCW; Part B: recommended guidance regarding provisions of the STCW convention and its annex.

4. What training should every crewmember have before working on board?

Basic safety training: basic fire prevention and fighting, basic first aid, basic safety, personal safety and social responsibilities.

5. Are the seafarers compulsory to be trained or qualified to carry out their duties on board the ship?

Yes, they are. Seafarers are not permitted to work on a ship unless they are trained or certified as competent or otherwise qualified to perform their duties.

注:船员必须经过培训,并持证上岗。

6. What special certificates should you have before working on oil tankers?

Endorsement of Special Training on Oil Tanker Familiarization 油轮船员特殊培训(安全知识)合格证; Endorsement of Special Training on Tanker Operation 油轮船员特殊培训(安全操作)合格证; Endorsement of Special Training on IGS and COW of Oil Tanker(油轮船员特殊培训(原油洗舱)合格证).

7. What position is added according to STCW 2010 Manila Amendments?

ETO(Electronic Technical Officer)电子员.

注:电子员应掌握电子海图显示与信息系统(ECDIS)、综合驾驶台系统(IBS)、全球海上遇险与安全系统(GMDSS)、数字调速器、机舱数据检测系统、电子主机及船舶局域网等船用电子设备与系统的有关知识与技术。

8. Which part of STCW is mandatory?

Part A.

9. When did Manila Amendments come into force?

Jan. 1, 2012 under the tacit acceptance procedures.

Part II Topics

1. What abilities should a C/E possess?

I think it's very important for a C/E to be skillful and proficient at work, he should maintain good management in the Engine Department. He should be able to motivate every person under his management by assigning jobs fairly among them. He also needs to be good in English and language communication. He should also maintain good relationship with the master, the technical superintendent and other personnel from the company.

2. What safety precautions should be taken in the E/R?

When welding, we should remove combustible materials. No smoking in the engine room. When working alone, we should keep in touch with other persons. Before entering the enclosed space, we should test the content of the oxygen and explosives, wear breathing apparatus and keep in touch with other persons. When blackout occurs, we should use the torch to avoid falling from height or bumping against something. Usually the checklist should be filled before the following work is carried out: welding, entering enclosed space, work at height, etc.

3. How do you practice and improve your English on board?

English is very important on board. If we cannot understand the orders in English, it may cause accidents. Also, we will go to some foreign countries to load and unload cargo, receive PSC inspection, do some shopping and visit some places. So we must learn English. We can read some English books, magazines and newspaper, browse on the internet of English. Listen to some English songs, watch some English films and news report. Try to be brave and speak aloud English. Never mind mistakes. Or you can write some letters or reports in English. Anyway we can learn English in many ways.

4. **What shall the engineering watch keeper know in addition to their assigned watchkeeping duties**?

（1）Knowledge of the use of appropriate internal communication system

（2）Knowledge of escape routes from the machinery space

（3）Knowledge of engine room alarm systems and the ability to distinguish between the various alarms with special reference to the CO_2 system

（4）Knowledge of the position and use of the fire fighting equipment in the machinery space.

4.7 海事劳工公约2006 International Maritime Labour Convention（IMLC）2006

Tips

2006 年国际海事组织出台了《海事劳工公约》。预计该公约除少数国家或地区不加入外，大多数国家都将加入，因此熟悉公约精神对维权、保护船员安全和个人权益是非常重要的。

Part I Questions

1. Is there any minimum age requirement on board?

Yes, any person under the age of 16 shall be prohibited and persons under the age of 18 shall be prohibited for night work.

注：16 岁以上工作合法，16 岁到 18 岁之间不得做夜班工作，中国海事局还对中国船员的年龄上做出规定，男性不得超过 65 岁，女性不得超过 60 岁。

2. What is the definition of night?

It covers at least nine hours starting no later than midnight and ending no earlier than 5 am.

3. Who will pay the cost of application and renewal of certificates such as national statutory medical certificate, the national seafarer's book and passport, cost of visas and so on?

According to IMLC, the shipowner may ask you to pay for those. However, the cost of visas is in the shipowner's account.

注:以国门为界线,凡是涉及出入境事宜,均由船东负责,如签证费、出国转船、住宿、飞机费用。国内段如职务证、健康证、海员证、体检等费用可以由船东出,也有可能要求船员出。

4. What is the maximum working hour for the seafarer according to 2006 International Maritime Labour Convention?

   14 hours in 24 hour period, or 72 hours in seven day period.

5. What is the minimum rest hours for the seafarer according to 2006 International Maritime Labour Convention?

   10 hours in 24 hour period, or 74 hours in seven day period.

6. What is the aim of 2006 International Maritime Labour Convention?

   To ensure that every seafarer has decent working condition and fair working condition and has the rights of health protection and social security.

4.8 船舶压载水和沉淀物控制和管理国际公约 International Convention for the Control and Management of Ships' Ballast Water and Sediments(BWM)

Tips

2004 年 2 月 13 日采纳,将在代表世界商船运量的 35% 的 30 个国家的同意后生效。各国应采取一切必要措施以防止、减少和控制由于在其管辖或控制下使用技术而造成的海洋环境污染,或由于故意或偶然在海洋环境某一特定部分引进外来的或新的物种致使海洋环境可能发生重大和有害的变化。船东有可能要测试船员对这方面知识的掌握情况。

Part I　Questions

1. What is the purpose of BWM?

   To minimize the transfer of harmful aquatic（水的）organisms and pathogens（病原体）by ballast water.

2. How much ballast water should be exchanged in volume?

   95%.

3. What is the leeway period for the prototype ballast water treatment technologies?

   Five years.

4. When will this convention come into effect?

   12 months after ratification by 30 states, representing 35% of world merchant shipping tonnage.

5. In order to limit the introduction of alien species（物种）from ship, what convention was adopted 13 Feb, 2004 at the IMO?

   International Convention for the Control and Management of Ships' Ballast Water and Sediments.

6. What methods are used to treat ballast water?

   Biocides, organisms, and biological mechanisms.

   注：biocides 生物杀灭剂，organisms 生物，有机体，biological mechanisms 生物学的机制。

7. What method is used to exchange ballast water?

   Pumping-through method.

Chapter 5   Professional Knowledge about Marine Engineering

第 5 章   轮机业务知识

5.1   主机 Main engine

Tips

主机即船用内燃机,为船舶航行提供动力,其良好的运行关系到船舶的行驶是否安全。因此,作为一名船员,对主机的了解,一定是最基本也是最重要的。

Part Ⅰ   Questions

1. What kind of main engine do you know?

   Sulzer, MAN B & W.

2. What is the main function of the governor of the main engine?

   Adjust the speed of main engine by adjusting fuel supply.

3. What is the function of the tie rods used in marine diesel engine?

   Hold the bedplate, A-frames and cylinder block together.

4. When selecting a fuel oil, there are more than ten factors to be considered. Please name at least three of the main factors.

   Among them are fuel oil's viscosity, cetane number, calorific value, the sulphur in it and ash.

5. A marine diesel engine consists of two parts. What are they?

   Moving parts and fixed parts.

6. What is called a working cycle of a marine diesel engine?

The operation between two injections is called a cycle.

7. Why is the two-stroke engine widely used as the main engine on board ship?

Because it theoretically develops twice the power of a four-stroke engine of the same size.

8. What is the sequence of the four strokes in a four-stroke diesel engine?

Suction, compression, expansion and exhaust.

9. What's called the stroke?

The stroke is the movement between TDC and BDC.

10. What should you usually do on the M/E?

We should maintain and repair it. Sometimes, we do maintenance work with the shipyard engineer.

11. The starting air pressure is too low. What should you do?

We should start the air compressor and pump up the air receiver.

12. What does the term "gas exchange" imply in the marine diesel engine?

It means the charging of fresh air and blowing out of exhaust gas.

13. How do you operate the main engine in cold weather?

First we should warm up the engine before starting it. After starting it, we should keep it running at a low speed, and then increase the engine speed gradually.

14. Could you tell me the main reason when you see the yellow smoke exhausting from the diesel engine?

There is too much sulphur in the fuel oil.

15. What do CPP and VPP stand for?

CPP stands for Controllable Pitch Propeller and VPP stands for Variable Pitch Propeller.

16. If the exhaust temp. is too high, what should you do as an engineer?

I should try to slow down the engine speed and find out the trouble if possible.

17. How do you check the engine telegraph?

Checking the engine telegraph usually begins with slow ahead, and then half ahead, full ahead, then return to "stop" or "finished with engine", then slow astern and so on.

18. How do you test main engine?

Inform the bridge that engine room would like to turn engine over slowly on air. Then give the engine a brief trial on power ahead and astern(engine tried out both ahead and astern).

19. How are you going to change fuel oil over to diesel oil?

Lower the temperature of the fuel to a proper temperature, then open the diesel oil valve and close the fuel oil valve, at the same time, keep close watch on the fuel system pressure to avoid low pressure.

20. Why does the engine speed rise up by using fuel oil instead of diesel oil?

Because the amount of fuel oil supplied is increased as a result of its higher calorific value and greater specific gravity.

21. When the fuel is provided by the supplier, what specifications of the oil can you get from the supplier's receipt?

The following information of the fuel shall be available: density, viscosity, temperature as delivered, water content, flash point and so on.

22. What shall we have to do with fuel when the ship is sailing in the cold zone?

When sailing in the cold zone, we should always warm up the oil storage tanks, fuel transfer piping, settling tank, and service tank.

23. What is the working stroke?

The expansion stroke.

24. In which cases must the main engine be stopped?

When the crankcase or scavenge explosion happens; when the oil pipe is broken and a great deal of oil is spilled out; when the running of the diesel engine has been of great danger to the safety of crew or will cause a major accident.

25. The engine may lose power or slow down when running. What is the possible cause?

The cause may be hot bearings and seizure of the pistons in the cylinders(咬缸) etc.

26. What kind of precaution will you take to avoid a crankcase explosion?

We should check the temperature and level of lube oil in the crankcase carefully. We should also keep the ventilator opening.

27. Do you know the ME and MC engines in MAN B&W Company?

Yes, the ME means electronic-controlled engines, and MC means camshaft-controlled ones.

28. Among the 4 strokes, which one can provide the ship with driving power?

Among the 4 strokes, only the expansion stroke provides the ship with driving power, so it is also called power stroke.

29. What are the speed ranges of the diesel engines?

Low, medium and high speed diesel engines are respectively below 300 rpm, between 300 and 1,200 rpm, and above 1,200 rpm.

30. What are the usual applications of diesel engines on board ship?

The two-stoke crosshead low speed type diesel engines are used as main engine on board ship, and the four-stroke trunk piston medium speed type diesel engines are used as auxiliary engines, but sometimes they are used as main engines.

31. What are the main systems included in the main engine?

The cooling system, the lubrication system, the fuel oil system, the turbo charging system, the starting system and the operating system.

32. What are the usual coolants used on board ship?

The usual coolant is fresh water. Lubricating oil is sometimes used for piston cooling since leaking into the crankcase would not cause problem. Seawater cannot be used directly as coolant because of its corrosive action, but it is used to cool fresh water.

33. What is the function of cooling system?

Cooling system is used to cool various parts in order to retain the mechanical property of metal as well as to prolong their trouble-free time.

34. What are the two cooling water systems on board ship?

The open sea water cooling system, and closed fresh water cooling system.

35. What are the advantages of central cooling system?

The central cooling system has replaced the traditional cooling system, which has several advantages such as to simplify(简化) the cooling water piping, lessen(减轻) the maintenance of cooling system and much reduce the corrosive action of sea water.

36. Why do we use lubricating oil to cool piston?

If we use water to cool piston, the lube oil in the crankcase will be polluted by leaking water, but lubricating oil won't cause such pollution.

37. What is the function of head tank?

Head tank is also called expansion tank, it has four functions: to hold the expansion of water due to the increase of temperature, to make up for the water which has evaporated or been otherwise lost, to release excess air, and to purify water by chemical addition.

38. What are the lubricants used on board ship?

Lubricating oil and grease.

39. What are the duties of lubricating oil?

To provide lubricating films, to remove heat from oil cooled pistons, to neutralize acidic products of combustion, to cleanse hot moving parts of carbonaceous deposits, to resist oxidation and to wash away wear detritus.

40. What is the function of the fuel oil system?

Fuel oil has much to do with the operation as well as maintenance of an engine, which means that without fuel oil system an internal combustion engine can't work at all.

41. What are usual fuels used on board ship?

Diesel oil and fuel oil. We use diesel oil when the ship is in maneuvering condition.

42. How do you distinguish diesel oil and fuel oil?

Diesel oil and fuel oil have different applications on board. Diesel oil is used when the ship is in maneuvering condition. And they are different in specific gravity, viscosity, flash point and calorific value.

43. What does fuel oil system include?

The whole fuel oil system includes bunkering, storage, treatment, supply and injection, etc.

44. What are the two sub-systems in fuel oil system?

They are fuel supply and fuel injection system.

45. What is the relationship between viscosity and temperature?

The higher the temperature of oil is, the lower its viscosity becomes, and vise versa.

46. Before entering the cylinder, fuel oil should receive some treatment, what are they?

Fuel oil should be heated, settled, purified, filtered, and pressurized before injecting into the cylinder.

47. What equipment do we usually use to purify oil?

The oil separator or centrifuge.

48. What is the working principle of purifier?

Under centrifugal force, water and impurities in the oil will be separated because of density differential.

49. Why are there some heating pipes in the fuel oil system?

The heating pipe is used to heat the fuel oil inside the fuel lines, in this case, the viscosity can be low enough for it to flow smoothly.

50. What is the viscosity regulator used for?

The viscosity regulator is used to regulate the viscosity of fuel oil by heating it, in order to provide combustion with oil in correct viscosity.

51. In what state is the fuel oil injected into the cylinder?

The fuel oil when being injected into the cylinder should be in fine spray.

52. What is the purpose of turbo charging?

Turbo charging is to increase inlet air volume, thus promoting more complete and clean combustion.

53. What is the structure of turbocharger?

The turbocharger has on opposite ends of a single shaft, an exhaust gas driven turbine and an air compressor. The two are sealed from each other.

54. What is scavenging?

Scavenging means removing exhaust gas by blowing in fresh air.

55. Do you know the importance of scavenging?

I think there are two effects of scavenging, one is the cylinder can be adequately cleared of gases, further, the air inlet temperature would be cool enough.

56. What is volumetric efficiency(容积效率)?

Volumetric efficiency is the ratio of volume of air drawn into a cylinder to the piston displacement volume, which indicates the efficiency of suction, the higher the better.

注:增压越高,同样容积下可更多地吸入空气,使燃烧更充分,或多喷油,多做工。

57. What are the symptoms of scavenging fire?

High exhaust temperature, black smoke, engine speed slowing down automatically, surging of turbocharger, overheating and panting of scavenging air box, spark and fume emitting from the scavenging drain, etc.

58. If scavenging fire occurs, what may be the reasons?

Fouling of fuel injectors, poor atomizing, incomplete combustion, dirty scavenging air box, piston ring broken causing combustion gas entering the scavenging trunk, etc.

59. What measures should be taken to avoid scavenging fire?

To drain and clean scavenging air box regularly, to avoid overloading of main engine, regular inspection of injectors, regular examination of liners and piston rings, etc.

60. How is diesel engine started?

Diesel engine is started by providing cylinder with compressed air at the right moment in correct sequence.

61. What is starting air and pilot air?

Starting air means the compressed air that pushes the piston to do work on the crankshaft. Pilot air means the compressed air that controls various valves.

62. If the main engine exhausts black smoke, what may be the reasons?

There are several reasons such as overloading, incomplete combustion, incorrect timing of injection advanced angle, poor atomizing, etc.

63. What's wrong if the main engine emits blue smoke when operating?

The reason may be large sum of lubricating oil enters combustion chamber.

64. What will critical speed of diesel engine lead to?

The speed at which serious vibration and noise of diesel engine occurs.

65. What is engine telegraph?

Telegraph is a communication device used between the bridge and engine room to confirm the speed and direction of the main engine.

66. How long is it between an overhaul?

Approximately 8,000—10,000 hours. It may vary in different types of machines.

67. How do you know it is 8,000 hours?

We can look it up in the log of the machine.

68. Who decides the overhaul?

Chief Engineer decides it. Captain should be reported, because we need to stop engine while overhaul.

Part II Topics

1. Is there any difference between the diesel engine and the gasoline engine?

The fundamental difference between gasoline and diesel engine is that in the gasoline engine the source of the heat for igniting the charge is the electric sparks. The diesel engine is somewhat less complex in design than the gasoline engine because it does not require an ignition system to ignite the fuel charge. A diesel engine compared with the same size gasoline engine produces somewhat greater torque or is more efficient and produces less harmful exhaust emissions. The diesel engine operates on a somewhat less expensive fuel.

2. Please describe the lubricating mode of main engine.

Large marine diesel engines of crosshead construction generally have two systems of lubrication: a total loss system feeding the cylinders and a circulating system lubricating the running gear and cooling the pistons. In the total loss system, oil is injected between the liner and the piston by mechanical lubricators which supply their individual cylinder. A special type of oil is used which is not recovered. In the circulating system, the lubricating oil for an engine is stored in the bottom of the crankcase, known as the sump, or in a drain tank located beneath the engine. The oil is drawn from this tank through a strainer, one of a pair of pumps, into one of a pair of fine filters. It is then passed through a cooler before entering the engine and being distributed to the various branch pipes to lubricate the different running parts. After use in the engine the lubricating oil drains back to the sump or drain tank for reuse.

3. Introduce the equipment and machinery in the engine room.

The main engine is the most important equipment on board. It usually consists of cylinders, pistons, crankshafts, main bearings, connecting rods, cooling system, starting system, lubricating system and operating system. Auxiliary machines are much more in number, but not as large as the main engine. Some deck machinery also belongs to them. They are generators, boilers, fresh water generators, refrigerating plant, all kinds of pumps and so on. They are indispensable for the operation of a ship. According to the numbers of strokes, the marine engine can be divided into two kinds, 2-stroke and 4-stroke diesel engines.

4. What should be prepared before disassembly of cylinder for main engine/auxiliary engine?

I shall familiarize myself with the operational manual, such as know with certainty the disassembly procedures, cut off oil and water, test by oil and water after assembly; get knowledge of assembly crevice(裂缝;裂隙) and limited crevice; count on necessary spares; check all necessary tools before working; make clear duties for personal engagement in disassembly of cylinder; safety measures and safety working training are also vital.

5. Actions to be taken in the case of trial of main engine.

Before testing, he should ensure that the turning gear is disengaged, and all systems in the main engine in good operation. Close the indicator cock; open the outlet valve for the air receiver. Ensure that the main engine can start with no difficulties of engine shafting systems. Put the telegraph handle to "Dead Slow Ahead". Then the bridge gives telegraph orders after the bow and stern being all clear, at that time the duty engineer can start the trial of engine.

6. Actions to be taken in the event of the turbocharger surge.

In the event of the turbocharger surge, we should report it to the chief engineer immediately.

Regulate its revolution further to avoid continuous surging. Then, we should avoid severe or even dangerous vibration. Finally, in order to sail safely we should be more careful. We should record it in the engine room log book.

7. Notice to be taken when the main engine running with one cylinder being cut off.

When the main engine running with one cylinder being cut-off, first, we should prevent the diesel engine from being overloaded. In order to achieve that, we can reduce its revolution. Secondly, if the turbocharger surges, regulate its revolution further to avoid continuous surging. Thirdly, we should avoid severe or even dangerous vibration. Finally, in order to sail safely we should be more careful. If anything abnormal happens, we should report it to the chief engineer immediately.

8. What should be done if scavenging fire occurs?

The duty engineer should slow down the main engine, increase lubricating, cut off the affected cylinder; but if the fire burns heavily, the duty engineer should stop the main engine, and put out fire with steam and cool it with water. The scavenging air box should be opened after cooling down.

Commonly used phrases

two-stroke engine 两冲程主机

camshaft-less 无凸轮轴

common rail 共轨

VIT 可变喷油定时

scavenging fire 扫气箱着火

crankcase explosion 曲柄箱爆炸

5.2 发电机 Generator

Tips

发电机通常采用的是四冲程柴油机作为原动机,为船舶的主要用电设备提供电源。在紧急情况下,应急发电机或者是蓄电池也可以作为船上的用电电源。

Part I Questions

1. According to the speed, how are the engines classified?

The low speed engine, medium speed engine, and high speed engine.

2. What is the main power supply in docking repair?

Shore power supply.

3. What is the function of the emergency generator?

It is to supply power to the critical equipment on board ship in an emergency condition in case of the main power failure.

4. What are the different ways by which it is possible to start the emergency generator?

In terms of battery, air or hand-cranking.

5. How do you know the wire should be renewed?

Choose any band in random. If there is more than 10% of the wire chosen damaged, the whole wire should be changed.

6. Where is the emergency generator located?

It is located outside of the machinery space.

7. Who is in charge of emergency generator?

The second engineer.

8. What is the emergency source of electrical power on board?

Emergency generator or battery.

9. What equipment should be first provided with electricity by emergency generator?

The navigational aids, lighting, communication system, a ventilating fan in the E/R and the steering gear should be first provided with electricity.

10. In the event of blackout, what should you do at first as a duty engineer?

I should inform the chief engineer at once and then start the spare generator group.

11. In the event of blackout, what should you do as a chief engineer?

I should enter the engine room at once and ask engineers to find out the trouble and repair it as soon as possible.

12. What will the accumulation of dirt on electrical equipment result in?

Insulation breakdown, leakage current and even earth fault.

13. Please describe the component of the ship power plant.

   Power station, switchboard, and electrical load.

14. How often do you test batteries and charger?

   Every week.

15. How many methods are generally available to start the emergency generator?

   Manual/electric/hydraulic/starting compressed air.

16. What does the whole electrical system on board include?

   It is composed of generators, power distribution system and electrical equipment.

17. How many generators are there on board ship?

   Usually there are at least three generators on board—one used as main generator, one used as standby ones, and an emergency generator. If electricity demand is large, there is usually a shaft generator onboard some ships.

18. What is shaft generator?

   Shaft generator is powered by the main engine, it is to offer additional power for the ship.

19. What provides driving power for generators?

   Generators are driven by diesel engines, so they can also be called diesel generators or auxiliary engines, or by steam turbine.

20. How is current produced?

   A coil of wire rotating in a magnetic field produces current.

21. What is an open circuit?

   An electric circuit that has been broken, so that there is no complete path for current flow.

22. What is a short circuit?

   A short circuit is simply a low resistance connection between the two conductors supplying electrical power to any circuit. This results in excessive current flow.

23. How is circuit connected?

Circuit can be connected in series or in parallel.

24. What are the usual electrical instruments?

Ammeter, voltmeter, ohmmeter, wattmeter, frequency meter, synchroscope, and so on.

Part II Topics

1. Describe the procedure to start an emergency generator.

(1) Check the lube oil level in the crankcase and fuel oil level in the tank all at normal level.

(2) Check to see if there is any leakage.

(3) Make sure there aren't any obstacles around the machine.

(4) Put the test switch in "Manual" position, and manually start it after making sure that above-mentioned items in order.

(5) "Auto test" must be carried out once every month. "Black-out" test must be carried out once every 3 months.

2. Describe the maintenance work of emergency battery.

Battery maintenance is substantially the same for both types of battery. Cell tops must be kept clean and dry, vents clear and free from deposits, terminal connections tight, free of corrosion and coated with petroleum jelly to prevent corrosion. Electrolyte levels should be checked and topped up with distilled water to cover the plates.

3. What actions should be taken when black-out occurs?

First, we should inform the bridge and start up the stand-by generator automatically to supply power. Secondly, we must take care not to fall from high point or hit objects because visibility decreases. Thirdly, we should try to find the cause for blackout. Finally, as normal operation recovers, inform the bridge, stop the emergency generator engine and record in the engine log book.

Commonly used phrases

power station 电站(power generating unit)

switchboard 配电板(power distribution unit)

electrical load 电负荷(power utilizing unit)

battery 电池

5.3 辅机 Auxiliary machinery

Tips

船舶辅机包括锅炉、泵、阀、舵机、甲板机械、锅炉、分油机等,它们都为船舶的安全行驶和主机的正常运行提供了重要的保障。这一部分无论是在专业上还是在英语学习中都是比较复杂的,需要轮机员掌握全面而且完善的知识,才能应对面试中的问题。

Part I Questions

1. What is the commonly used boiler?

   The exhaust boiler and the oil-burning boiler.

2. What boiler is used on a motor ship when at sea?

   Exhaust gas boiler, or waste heat boiler.

3. What boiler is used on a motor ship when in port?

   Oil-burning boiler.

4. Why do you carry out the water treatment for the boiler?

   Because feed water and boiler water treatment must be maintained to prevent internal deterioration or scale formation.

5. What's the function of an exhaust gas boiler?

   It is used to recover the heat from the M/E thus improving the plant efficiency.

6. What are the typical parts of boiler on board ship?

Steam drum, water drum, air draught fan, fuel burner, oil heater, fresh water pump, steam condenser, superheater, downcomer tubes, generating tubes, etc.

7. What is the common trouble of a boiler?

There will be scale on the steam generating side, failure of ignition, etc.

8. Why is it important to clean the fireside of the boiler periodically?

The soot on the fireside will reduce the heat exchange efficiency. And dirty boiler tubes cause smoking and when soot collections on the tubes, overheating of the superheater will result.

9. How do you clean the waterside boiler?

There are two methods to clean: chemical tube cleaner and boiling out with suitable chemical compounds.

10. When does a boiler discharge residue, at low load or high load?

Low load.

11. What's the type of the fuel oil separator?

The purifier and clarifier.

12. What's the function of the fuel oil separator?

It's to treat the fuel oil and remove water and impurities from fuel oil.

13. What's the type of oily water separator?

The gravity-separating type and the gravity-separating combined with coalescence, filtering or absorption types.

14. What is the function of the oily water separator?

It is used to ensure that ships do not discharge oil overboard in order to prevent oil pollution.

15. What is the function of the soot-blower?

It is used to blow away soot and products of combustion from the tube surface.

16. What type is the most common marine refrigeration?

The compression refrigeration.

17. What equipment is used to handle the anchor?

Windlass.

18. What's the function of the incinerator?

It's used to burn out oil sludge.

19. When must you test the steering gear?

When the ship is going to sail, before arriving port, after the ship has an overhaul or the ship has just stood the test of rough sea.

20. What's the type of fresh water generator?

The vacuum boiling evaporator and flash evaporator.

21. Please name at least 3 items of deck machinery.

Cargo winch, windlass, mooring winch, hydraulic hatch cover, etc. .

22. How do you clean the disc of an oil separator?

I clean the disc of the oil separator with diesel oil or specific detergent.

23. What type is the F. O. transfer pump?

It is a gear pump.

24. What type is the F. W. transfer pump?

It is a centrifugal pump.

25. What type is the S. W. transfer pump?

It is a centrifugal pump.

26. What type is the D. O. transfer pump?

It is a gear pump.

27. What type of pump is gear/reciprocating pump?

It is a positive displacement pump.

28. What pumps belong to the centrifugal pump?

It is the turbine pump/volute pump/diffuser pump/mixed-flow pump/axial-flow pump and so on.

29. Do you know the types of gear pump?

They are the spur gear pump(正齿轮泵), and helical gear pump(斜齿轮泵).

30. What's the function of the steering gear?

To provide a rudder movement to control the ship's course.

31. What is the anchor winch used for?

The anchor winch or windlass is used to drop or heave in the anchor through the hawse pipe. The anchor chain is stored in the chain locker.

32. What's a condenser for the steam system? And what is its function?

Condenser is an auxiliary equipment used for the cooling purpose. It is an apparatus for converting exhaust steam to water by means of heat transfer. Its function is to transfer heat steam into water.

33. Do you know some types of refrigerant?

Refrigerant 12, 22, 502, etc.

34. Can you list basic components of the refrigeration plant?

Compressor, condenser, expansion valve, evaporator and liquid receiver.

35. Do you know the types of the compressor?

The reciprocating compressor, the centrifugal compressor and screw compressor.

36. What should you periodically do for the air reservoir?

We should drain the air reservoir periodically.

37. How do you fill Freon 22 into the refrigeration system?

Through the charging valve fitted before the expansion valve.

38. Who should be present when a boiler survey is carried out?

Chief engineer, the engineer in charge of the boiler, and the Class surveyor.

39. What is the working principle of the centrifugal pump?

Centrifugal pump is a pump in which the high rotating impeller throws the liquid from center to the periphery by centrifugal force.

40. What is the function of the centrifugal pump?

Centrifugal pump is used for delivering large quantities at low pressure.

41. What are the two types of boiler?

Fire-tube boiler and water-tube boiler.

42. What is used for cargo handling?

Crane or cargo winch.

43. What is SWL of the crane?

Safe Working Load(安全负荷量).

Part II　Topics

1. Talk about the working principle of oily water separator.

Oily water separators using gravity system can only achieve 100 ppm, it must be used together with some form of filter to discharge clean water less than 15 ppm of oil. Oily water separator is first filled with clean water and the oily water mixture is then pumped through the separator inlet pipe into the coarse separating compartment. Here some oil will separate and rise into the oil collection space. The remaining oil/water mixture now flows down into the fine separating compartment and moves slowly between the catch plates. More oil will separate out onto the underside the plates and travel outwards until it is free to rise into the oil collection space. Then the almost oil-free water passes into the central pipe and leaves the separator unit from the oil outlet.

2. What is the usual anti-pollution equipment on board the ship?

In order to prevent pollution by oil from ships, we have to

comply with MARPOL Convention 73/78. On board the ship, oily water separators are used to ensure that ships do not discharge oil when pumping out bilge water, oily water from oil tanks or any other oil contaminated spaces. Incinerators are used to burn out oil sludge and wastes. Sometimes we can also discharge oily water to the shore reception facilities.

3. Do you know anything about the ballast system?

The ballast system is used to pump water into or from the sea or any tank to trim the vessel. First we have to get the written permission from the bridge. Before starting pumps, we should make sure that there is no electric overload. Pumps should be started in a closed system, valves should be in correct position, and water level should be checked frequently by the bridge. The engine department will stop the operation according to the bridge's instructions.

4. Talk about the operation of the bilge system.

The bilge water system is used to collect, store or discharge the oily water accumulated in the machinery space. The fourth engineer is in charge of the bilge operation. He should get the written permission from the deck department; oily water separator should be put into operation and oil content in the discharge water should be less than 15 ppm. When the separator is stopped, it should be flushed with clean fresh water for about half an hour.

5. Talk about steering gear testing.

Before a ship's departure from any port, the steering gear should be tested by remote control from the bridge. The rudder angle indicator reading should be respected to the actual rudder. Both main and auxiliary steering gear should be operated using the emergency power supply and alarms should be checked for correct operation. During the test, the rudder should be removed through its full travel in both directions and the various equipment items, linkages, etc., visually inspected for damage or wear. The communication system between the bridge and the steering gear should also be operated.

Commonly used phrases

　　mixed-flow pump 混流泵

　　axial-flow pump 轴流泵

　　helical gear pump 螺旋齿轮泵

　　refrigerant 制冷剂

　　crane 克令吊,起重机

5.4　轮机自动化 Ship's automation

Tips

　　随着航运事业的发展,技术的不断革新,船舶上的自动化程度越来越高。自动化程度越高,对船舶电气和轮机自动化控制要求就越高。

Part I　Questions

1. What does UMS stand for?

　 It means Unmanned Machinery Space/Unattended Machinery Space(无人机舱).

2. What is the IC?

　 IC stands for the integrated circuit(集成电路).

3. What is the LSIC?

　 LSIC stands for large scale integrated circuit(大规模集成电路).

4. What is the VLSIC?

　 VLSIC stands for very large scale integrated circuit(超大规模集成电路).

5. What is the ULSIC?

　 ULSIC stands for ultra large scale integrated circuit(巨大规模集成电路).

6. Do you know the types of the basic logic gate circuits?

They include AND, OR, NOT logic circuits(AND "与"OR"或" NOT"非"电路中的逻辑关系)

7. What are the two logic gate circuits?

O level and 1 level or low voltage level and high voltage level.

8. What automation does your ship have?

The chief engineer is able to watch all parameters in his cabin. The engine room is unmanned when the ship sails.

9. How often do you carry out a Megger(兆欧表)test?

Quarterly.

10. How do you know the characteristics of an integrated circuit?

It depends on the manufacture. In general, the reference book introduces the function of an integrated circuit.

11. Can you give me some examples of closed loop control?

Bridge control of main engine, steering gear control, boiler control, cargo control and so on.

12. What is the function of feedback?

This is the transmission of a signal representing the output for comparison with the input to the system. Feedback can increase accuracy.

13. What are the most sophisticated control and most simple one?

The simplest control is on-off control(two-step control 双位控制). The most sophisticated one is PID control(比例加微分加积分控制).

14. What is ETO?

Electronic Technical Officer. It is a new position on board to comply with the STCW 2010 Manila Amendments.

Part Ⅱ　Topics

Describe UMS

UMS stands for Unattended Machinery Space. The sophistication and reliability of modern equipment results in UMS. In this control process, the computer can supervise the operation of machinery, record the operation, and make necessary adjustment. The bridge can take control of the main engine when the engine room is unattended overnight. If emergency conditions occur, the designated engineer will be notified immediately.

Commonly used phrases

AND "与" OR "或" NOT "非" 电路中的逻辑关系

Megger test 高阻表测试

electrolyzed solution 电解液

UMS(unattended machinery space) 无人机舱

Chapter 6　Crew's Duties and Knowledge about Engine Room Resources Management

第6章　船员职责与机舱资源管理知识

6.1　各级船员基本职责 Basic duties of all levels

Tips

各级船员应熟悉自己的日常工作、职责,尤其是应急情况下的职责。这也是船东面试中经常涉及的话题。

Part Ⅰ　Questions

1. What is the main duty of the C/E?

He is responsible for the management of the engine department and safe operation of all equipment in the engine department. He is responsible for the master.

注:也可这样回答 The Chief Engineer is ultimately responsible for the safe and efficient running of all mechanical and electric machinery(responsible for all operations and maintenance that has to do with any and all engineering equipment throughout the entire ship.)

2. What is the main duty of the 2/E?

The Second Engineer is responsible for watching at periods of 0400—0800 hours and 1600—2000 hrs. He is responsible to the

Chief Engineer for the operation and maintenance of all machinery and associated equipment. Operational duties include responsibility for the refrigeration systems, main engines(steam/gas turbine, diesel), and any other equipment not assigned to the Third Engineer. Also, he is responsible for PMS.

注:计划维修保养体系(Planned Maintenance System, PMS)的知识。几乎所有的大公司都建有 PMS 系统,以统筹全船机电设备的维修、检验与管理,轮机长是技术总负责人。轮机人员要非常熟悉机器的维修保养工作及相关问题,熟悉 PMS 软件系统的操作。

3. What is the main duty of the 3/E?

Keep watch from 0000 to 0400 both in the morning and in the evening. He is usually in charge of boilers, fuel, auxiliary engines, condensate, and feed systems.

4. What is the main duty of the 4/E?

He is usually responsible for electrical, sewage treatment, lube oil, bilge, and oily water separation systems.

5. What is your first responsibility at all times when keeping watch in the engine room?

To maintain safe operating conditions, safe working practice and good housekeeping.

注:机舱值班时,第一个职责是维护机器的安全有效操作,安全工作惯例和良好的管理。

6. What action will you take if you get the "low lube oil pressure" alarm for the main engine?

The features of L. O. are to reduce friction in order to decrease the temperature. So if the L. O. feeding drops, I shall immediately take measures, otherwise it may cause machinery damage or even a fire or explosion. I shall inform the bridge and my chief engineer. I shall check the cause of the low L. O.

pressure and start the backup L. O. pump. I shall check the second strainer.

注:润滑油油压过低报警后,应检查原因,起动备用的润滑油泵,检查第二级滤器。

7. What action will you take in case of blackout?

Stop main engines—inform bridge—start another generator.

注:blackout 全船失电。

8. What are the duties of the No. 1 motorman/No. 1 oiler? (机工长)

Under the direction of the chief engineer or the second engineer, the No. 1 motorman organizes the arrangement of watchkeeping of the motormen in navigation and in port. In accordance with the planned maintenance and repair work and under direction of the second engineer, the No. 1 motorman arranges the maintenance and repair work. If there is no storeman on board, the No. 1 motorman should account and manage tools, spare parts, and stores and record those in books if there is no storeman on board the ship. The No. 1 motorman should fulfill other work assigned by the chief engineer or second engineer.

9. What are the responsibilities of the motorman? (机工)

Under the duty engineer and the No. 1 motorman, a motorman should take charge of observance of watchkeeping and operational manuals. A motorman should manage the running of all machinery and electrical equipment, attend routine maintenance and repair work, and fulfill other work assigned by the second engineer or the No. 1 motorman.

10. What are the responsibilities of the wiper? (清洁工)

The wiper takes charge of cleaning the engine room. The wiper is also responsible for maintenance and repair work assigned by the chief engineer, second engineer, and duty engineer. The wiper takes charge of oil cleaning work in the engine room if there is oil leakage. The wiper takes charge of bilge water removal if the bilge water is found at the bottom of the engine room.

11. What are the responsibilities of the fitter? （焊工）

The fitter takes charge of maintenance and repair work, especially the welding operations. The fitter is also responsible for the other work assigned by the chief engineer, second engineer, or duty engineer. The fitter is also responsible for the work and safety prevention procedure in the workshop.

12. What are the responsibilities of the storeman? （士多）

The storeman is a person who keeps stores and spare parts in the engine room. The storeman must keep the account for stores and spare parts in the engine room. The storeman is required to keep good record when the stores and spare parts are applied for. When the position is transferred to relieving staff, the stores and spare parts are requested to be counted for record.

13. What is the status of the duty engineer?

The duty engineer is also called the officer in charge of the engineering watch. He is the representative of the chief engineer. He shall be responsible for the safe and efficient operation of the machines in the machinery space.

14. In what situation should the engineer not hand over the watch to the relieving engineer?

If the relieving officer is drunk or under the influence of liquor; the relieving engineer is sick or too weak to carry out the duties; the relieving engineer is under the influence of dangerous and prohibited drugs.

注:如发现接班人酗酒、生病,或者有吸毒倾向,交班人不应该交接,并立即向轮机长报告。

15. What will the relieving engineer check before handling over the duty?

He will check the engine room operating machinery, usually the main engine and their auxiliary equipment, including their systems, the bilge and steering room bilges; settling and daily service tanks level; previous and present entries entered in the engine logbook. He will ask the engineer being relieved whether the verbal orders are available or not.

16. What do you usually do when keeping watch?

I will tour in the engine room, checking the operations of main engine and auxiliary machinery and their systems and take sounding of the oil levels, temperatures and pressures of oil and water.

17. What do you record in the engine room log book?

I will note the temperature and pressures of oil, water, exhaust gas, quantity of oily water pumped out, location and so on.

18. When the deck informs you that the ship is entering fog area, what should you do as a duty engineer?

I will observe the orders of alteration of speed and direction from the bridge, and carry out the orders immediately. I will standby the engine, to ensure there is an adequate compressed air is available for sound signals at any time, the communication between the bridge and engine room is clear.

19. When the deck informs you that the ship is entering the coastal water, or congested water, what should you do as a duty engineer?

I will follow the orders from the bridge, like (1) standby engine; (2) use of manual operation from auto modes of operation; (3) to guarantee that steering gear system in good order; (4) preparation of emergency steering system and other machinery.

20. When you are in engine room as E. O. W. (值班轮机员), what are your first responsibilities at all times?

To maintain safe operating conditions, safe working practices and good house-keeping.

21. When taking over watch in the engine room, what should you do and what you should not do?

Always be fit for duty; always arrive in sufficient time to carry out a check of all machinery before taking over the watch; read, understand the C/E's standing orders and special instructions. If you are in any doubt, call the C/E immediately; complete the "Watch Handover" checklist or UMS checklist as applicable.

Part Ⅱ　Topics

If you work as a 4/E, tell me something about your duty

(1) Keep watch from 08:00 to 12:00 both A. M. and P. M..

(2) Be responsible for operation maintenance and repair of boiler, pumps, deck equipment, pollution prevention equipment, fresh water generator, emergency fire pump, emergency generator, life-boat engine, and so on.

(3) Carry out instructions relating to ballasting and deballasting.

(4) Assist the 3/E in all technical aspects.

Commonly used phrases

dense fog 浓雾

shallow water 浅水区

costal 沿岸

hand over/take over the watch 交班/接班

6.2　机舱资源管理 Engine Room Resources Management (ERRM)

Tips

伴随着工业自动化技术的日新月异的变化,船舶机舱自动化技术也有着突飞猛进的发展。随着机舱自动化水平的不断提高,机舱设备的集成度、稳定性、通用性也日益加强。然而,自动化技术的发展并没有给机舱安全带来质的变化。经过对船舶机损事故的整理分析,在国内主要航运公司发生的 400 多件重大机损案例中,人为因素失误的案例达 330 件,占全部案例的 83.1%,与国内外公认的 80% 的人为因素失误比率非常接近,证实了船舶事故在许多方面与人的因素有关,人为因素失误是船舶事故的最主要原因,因此从宏观角度对机舱资源进行整理分析,对于减少机舱人为因素失误很有意义。机舱资源管理体系主要从四个方面入手,包括机舱人力资源管理,机舱设备资源管理,机舱消耗资源管理,机舱信息资源管理。其中人力资源管理主要包含人为因素、安全文化、技术管理。机舱设备资源管理主要包含动力设备管理、管系管理。机舱消耗资源管理主要包含油类管理、备件物料管理、淡水管理。机舱信息资源管理主要包含机舱资料管理、日常维护管理。

Part I Questions

1. How will you be deemed as a good leader?

To familiarize workmanship, to get good knowledge of management, to communicate with his hands, and to have the ability of competent skills to perform his duties perfectly, and to cooperate well with other departments.

2. What is the relationship between the master and the chief engineer?

The master is the leader of the whole ship and the chief engineer is responsible for the engine department. The master should respect the chief engineer, since the chief engineer knows the management of engines and machineries. The master should trust chief engineer on maintenance and repair of machines. And the chief engineer should obey the instructions of the master. Anyway, navigation is a teamwork.

注:轮机长是船长的下级。但船舶管理实践中,轮机长和船长也是合作关系,船长对轮机长更多的是尊重和目标管理。

3. If a crewmember was suspected of drinking alcohol, how would you react?

I would verify with the test meter to test BAC. If BAC is more than the suggested figure, I would, no doubt, stop his work immediately and let the crew rest until the crew is totally awake. Of course, the crew will be fined. Normally, crewmembers are not permitted to drink alcohol 4 hours before his duty.

注:本着先安置、后处置的原则。BAC(blood alcohol content)血液酒精含量,通常给定值为 40 mg/100 ml.

4. If the subordinate did not obey your instruction and he did not consult with you, what would you do?

I will discuss the matter with the master and recommend dismissing him.

5. Do you know how files and documents are managed?

Yes, files and documents can be arranged alphabetically numerically. The arrangement of numbering can be based on the importance of sequences, namely the most important file or document is numbered starting from Letter AA or Number 01. In addition, the arrangement can be based on dates.

注:文件的管理主要有三种方式核对文件编号:按日期、按重要程度、按文件首字母排序。

6. How would you manage the documents if you received a message from the shipping company or the shipmaster?

I would peruse the content in more detail and copy one if the content requires me to deal with it immediately, the original one should be registered with date and title in the Name List of the Documents, and put into the file clips for future check.

注:在从船长或船务公司收到信息后,怎样进行文件管理可以看出轮机长的办公管理意识,收到文件及时处理并登记。File clips 文件夹,Name List of the Documents 文件清单。

7. Who do you represent when keeping watch in the engine room?

I represent the chief engineer when I take the watch.

8. When will an engineer in charge of watch call the chief engineer?

In case of serious situations or he is unsure of the action to take, in case of captain's orders, he should call the chief engineer.

9. During your watch a serious situation becomes apparent to you and you find you have no time to telephone the master or C/E as you have to take remedial action. What would you do?

Do not hesitate to sound the General Alarm.

10. When you are in the engine room as E. O. W. , whom do you represent?

I represent the chief engineer.

11. What are the common human errors?

Like drinking before duty, throw cigarette ends anywhere, do not observe company's rules and regulations.

Part II Topics

1. What must be borne in mind when handling over the watch?

We must come down to the engine control room 15 minutes before the time we shift watches. I shall ask the conditions of the engines. I shall read the readings and record all parameters with my duty motorman. I shall ask whether there are orders from the chief engineer. I shall check the engine logbook for any abnormalities or requirements.

2. As a chief engineer, when must you come down to the engine room?

In the following cases, I must go down to the engine room. (1) When standby engine; (2) The duty engineer or other staff in my department calls for help; (3) A noise is sounding out form the engine room; (4) The alarm sounds; (5) An emergency incurs, such as fire, flooding, grounding, explosion; (6) Critical operations shall be executed.

3. Can you say something about the elements of risk assessment?

The main elements of the risk assessment are: (1) to determine work activities before working; (2) to compare the occurrence of a near miss or even disaster when other ships are operated in a similar operation; (3) to assess the other factors, such as weather, currents and so on; (4) to determine safety meetings prior to work; (5) to prepare a work plan; (6) to decide persons to monitor the whole process; (7) to review after work.

Commonly used phrases

resources 资源

team work 团队合作

near miss 险情

factor 因素

review 回顾

附录1 面试实例

Examples of Shipowners' Interview for Students
Example 1
A—Ship owner   B—Student
B: Good morning.
A: Good morning. Sit down please.
B: Thank you.
A: Can you introduce yourself?
B: My name is XXX. I'm from a small village in Xuzhou. I'm a marine engineering student.
A: What subjects do you study in this college?
B: Our main subjects are: Main Propulsion Diesel Engine, Ship's Automation, Auxiliary Machinery, Marine Engineering English, Ship's Management and so on.
A: What do you usually do in your spare time?
B: I usually play basketball. Sometimes I search on the internet.
A: Do you know anything about our company? /Why do you choose our company?
B: Yes. I know that your company is of high reputation, paying much attention to the development of seafarers. I think I will have a good chance. /Your company is a big company having a long history. It owns more than 30 container ships.
A: What's the function of the oily water separator?
B: Oily water separator is used to separate oil from water before pumping out bilge water. It is an anti-pollution equipment.

A: Yes, you have done a good job.

B: Thank you for your time.

Example 2

A—Shipowner B—Student

A: Come in, please. Sit down.

B: Thank you.

A: Your name? Can I see your resume?

B: Sure. My name is XXX. This is my resume.

A: Oh. You have passed CET-6. Good. Why do you choose marine engineering as your major? It's hard work.

B: I come from a poor family. My parents want me to be a good engineer in the future. I can endure hard work.

A: Do you know the function of generators?

B: Generators are used to convert mechanical energy into electrical energy. So that we can get electric power to drive other machines, such as pumps, fans and so on.

A: How often should the emergency generator be checked?

B: Once every week.

A: Can you name some tools used in the engine room?

B: Screwdrivers, hammers, hydraulic spanners, pipe wrench, pliers and so on.

Examples of Ship owners' Interview for Engineers
Example 1

A—Ship owner B—Fourth engineer

B: Hi, good morning!

A: Hi, guy. Sit sown please and let me have a look at your resume.

B: Here you are.

A: You have been working on container ships. What main engine and auxiliary engine have you served?

B: I have served MAN B& W, Sulzer, and the auxiliary engines are commonly Yanmar.

A: Have you met with the emergency situations? How did you deal with them?

B: I met with the blackout one day when I was on duty. I started the emergency generator at once, inform the bridge and the C/E. When the lighting system was all right, we tried to find out the causes.

A: How did you pump out the bilge water?

B: Bilge water should be treated through the oily water separator and the oil content should be less than 15 ppm to prevent oil pollution.

A: Yes, you are right. Pollution prevention should be borne in mind. OK. So much for the interview.

B: Thank you for your kind attention.

Example 2

A—Ship owner   B—Chief engineer

B: Good morning, Sir.

A: Good morning. What position do you want to apply?

B: I want to work as a C/E for your company. This is my resume.

A: You have worked on many kinds of ships, you are an experienced man. Can you tell me what the most important thing is on board?

B: Safety is the most important thing, the safety of ship, machinery, crew, and cargo. Also, we should take some measures to ensure security.

B: Yes. How do you maintain the safety of the ship for your department?

A: We usually have a regular safety meeting, all the crew should attend it except the duty men. Every man should bear safety in mind, esp. when we are going to take bunkers, enter and leave a port, do welding, approach some sensible waters, and so on.

A: How to prevent human factors?

B: We should first ensure every crewmember have a good rest and good mood for work, have the safety training often about fire fighting, life-saving, search and rescue. Try to enhance the crew's sense of responsibility.

A: Do you think teamwork is important?

B: Of course. On board the ship, we should work as a team. We should not only monitor the safety of our own work, but also monitor the other's work. If someone does something not safe for work, we should point it out. Help each other and work as a team.

参考文献

[1] 高德毅. 港口国监督检查问答. 大连：大连海事大学出版社，
    2009
[2] 张晓峰. 船员应对船东面试实用英语（轮机部）. 大连：大连海
    事大学出版社，2008
[3] 张晓峰. 电子电气员英语. 大连：大连海事大学出版社，2012